W9-BYD-041

WYOMING

WYOMING BY ROAD

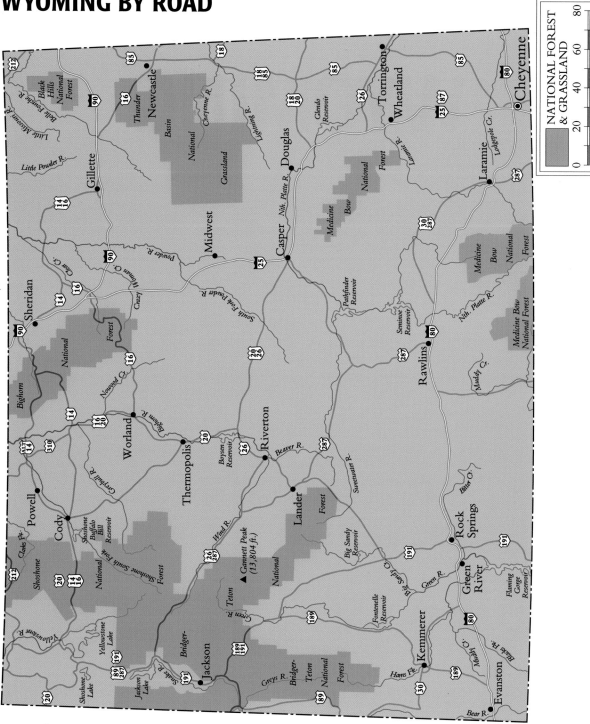

NATIONAL FOREST
& GRASSLAND

MILES

0   20   40   60   80

N
E
W
S

CELEBRATE THE STATES
WYOMING

Guy Baldwin

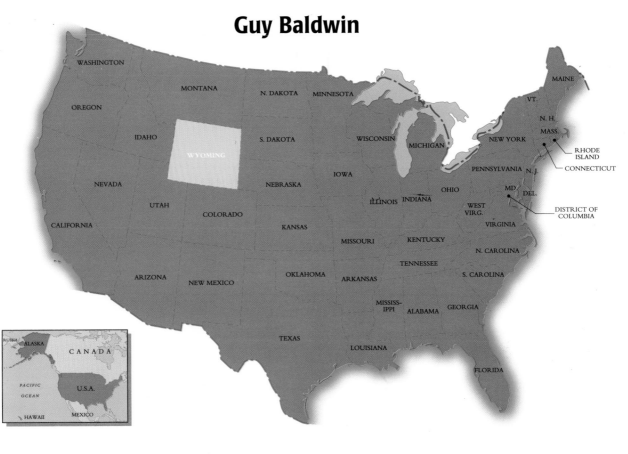

BENCHMARK BOOKS

MARSHALL CAVENDISH
NEW YORK

For Michelle Bennett

Benchmark Books
Marshall Cavendish Corporation
99 White Plains Road
Tarrytown, New York 10591-9001

Copyright © 1999 by Marshall Cavendish Corporation

Library of Congress Cataloging-in-Publication Data
Baldwin, Guy
Wyoming / Guy Baldwin.
p.   cm. —— (Celebrate the States)
Includes bibliographical references and index.
Summary: An overview of the geography, history, people,
and customs of the second-coldest state in the nation.
ISBN 0-7614-0662-X (lib. bdg.)
1. Wyoming—Juvenile literature. [1. Wyoming] I. Title. II. Series.
F761.3.B35   1999   978.7—dc21   97-38590   CIP   AC

Maps and graphics supplied by Oxford Cartographers, Oxford, England

Photo research by Ellen Barrett Dudley & Matthew Joseph Dudley

Cover photo: Wind River Photography

The photographs in this book are used by permission and through the courtesy of: *Jeff Vanuga*: 6-7, 19, 23, 63, 73, 78, 83, 84-85, 98-99, 103, 104(left), 114, 115, 125, backcover. *Ted Wood*: 10-11, 20, 56, 65, 66, 68-69, 76, 77, 81, 109, 116, 134. *Wind River Photography*: 13. *Photo Researchers, Inc.*: Francois Gohier, 14; Pat & Tom Leeson, 21; C. K. Lorenz, 22, 119(bottom); Jeff Lepore, 25; Fred J. Maroon, 50-51; J. P. Lenfant, 79; Mark Newman, 101; Anthony Mercieca, 119(top); Alan D. Carey, 122. *The Image Bank*: Steve Shatushek, 15; David W. Hamilton, 55; Peter Miller, 58; Geoffrey Gove, 105; Marvin E. Newman, 107. *Buffalo Bill Historical Center, Cody, WY*: 28-29; Gift of William E. Weiss, 31. *Wyoming Division of Cultural Resources*: 33, 35, 39, 40, 43, 44, 45, 88, 129(right), 133(top & bottom). *Torrington High School, Mural by Ernest Elmer Stevens, Photo by Richard Collier*: 34. *American Heritage Center, University of Wyoming*: 36. *U.S. Energy*: 48. *Department of the Air Force*: 57. *Montana Historical Society*: 87. *Corbis-Bettmann*: 91, 92, 129(left). *Archive Photos*: Kosta Alexander, 94. *AristoMedia*: 96. *Wyoming Travel Commission*: 118(bottom). *David Huber*: 128. *UPI/Corbis- Bettmann*: 130, 131, 132.

Printed in Italy

1   3   5   6   4   2

CONTENTS

WYOMING IS . . .

Wyoming is a land of secrets and surprises.

"So this was Wyoming, I thought, a secret, hidden world unknown to the rest of the country, serene and calm, with a slow heart beat."
—children's author Mary O'Hara

"The real secret of Wyoming's fascination is still basically *emptiness*. . . . Just to go along seeing nothing is a pleasure."
—writer Nathaniel Burt

It is home to hard workers . . .

"All of the kids at our school live on ranches. They know what hard work is. They have more responsibilities than a lot of adults do; they're helping their families survive every day. They have more business sense than any kids I've ever met."
—schoolteacher Kari Docktor

. . . who enjoy making do.

"One year, the snow was so deep early in the month that Maurice couldn't get up to the Bighorns to cut our customary Christmas tree, and we found a huge tumbleweed, sprayed it with glitter and decorated it."
—rancher Betty Evenson

Wyoming is a land of strong individuals . . .

"[A cowboy] was out fixing his fence one day when a tourist lady pulled up. 'Young man,' she said. 'I understand you have more cows than you do people out here. Why is that?' He looked at her with a steady gaze, hooked his thumb in his belt, and replied, 'We prefer 'em.'"   —Senator Alan Simpson

. . . who love their state.

"Whether natives or immigrants, Wyomingites treat the state as a treasured resource. . . . Most of Wyoming's people enjoy a love affair with space."

—University of Wyoming geographer Robert Harold Brown

Wyoming is a land of contrasts. It is the Cowboy State, where people celebrate the independence and self-reliance of Indians, ranchers, and pioneers. Yet these "rugged individualists" live in close, cooperative communities. It is the Energy State, too: its sprawling coal mines and oil fields supply power to the rest of the country. But it is also a place of undisturbed wilderness, of public lands preserved for everyone's enjoyment. Wyoming teems with wildlife but has fewer people than any other state. From its cities and towns to its mountaintops and canyons, Wyoming is a great place to live—and a fascinating place to explore.

1 A RUGGED WONDERLAND

Wyoming—a box on the map, measuring 275 miles north to south and 362 miles east to west. It's a box filled with treasure: majestic grasslands, soaring mountains, sparkling lakes, and rushing rivers. Besides the wondrous geology of Yellowstone, Flaming Gorge, and Devils Tower, there are swaying pine forests, severe desert basins, and a wealth of wildlife. It would be hard to draw this box anywhere else and come up with such spectacular contents.

GRASSLANDS AND MOUNTAIN RANGES

Wyoming is best known for its amazing mountains, but it is also a Great Plains state. Much of eastern Wyoming is rolling grassland broken by rocky outcrops. This region resembles neighboring areas of Montana, South Dakota, and Nebraska. The sky hangs like a blue tent over the land, and strong, steady winds toss the grass in rippling waves. Cattle and sheep graze the plains, and most of Wyoming's farms are here. There are few trees except along riverbanks. On most days, the clean, clear air allows people in eastern Wyoming to see for miles and miles.

South and west of the grasslands, Wyoming rises up in awe-inspiring mountain ranges. The Laramie Mountains in the state's southeastern corner include peaks that are over 10,000 feet tall. Higher still are the Medicine Bow and Bighorn Mountains in

Water is scarce on Wyoming's rich grasslands, but there's plenty of wind to power pumps that draw it out of the ground for thirsty livestock.

central Wyoming. But the tallest mountains are farther west, especially in the northwest corner of the state, where the Absaroka and Teton Ranges are found. The towering Grand Teton is 13,766 feet tall. But Wyoming's very highest mountain is Gannett Peak, which is farther south, in the Wind River Mountains. It is 13,804 feet tall—more than two and a half miles above sea level.

Though they are all part of the Rocky Mountains, each of these ranges is different. Some are the result of one plate in the earth's

The gorgeous Tetons have been called "the most photographed mountains in the world." They often appear as the background in movies that have nothing to do with Wyoming.

crust pushing another up from below. This raises the upper plate and creates "uplifted" mountains, like the Medicine Bow Range. Others, such as the Tetons, rose up because of volcanic pressure below the earth's surface. It is easy to see the difference. The layers of rock around uplifted ranges are tilted, so the mountains look like they were forced into the air from one side. The volcanic Tetons, by contrast, are shaped more like cones and push straight into the sky.

In the state's northwest corner, not far from the Tetons, is one of the most spectacular natural areas in the United States: Yellowstone National Park. Yellowstone sits on a "hot spot" where molten rock from the earth's interior has been driven almost to the surface. The heat it gives off produces hot springs, bubbling mudpots, and

Minerals that come from deep in the earth color hot springs like Yellowstone's Grand Prismatic Spring.

geysers—gushes of hot water that shoot into the air. Writer Rudyard Kipling was amazed by Yellowstone when he visited in 1910, calling it a "howling wilderness . . . full of all imaginable freaks of a fiery nature." Yellowstone serves as a refuge for many kinds of wildlife. It is one of the last places to find wild grizzly bears and bison.

Wyoming's mountain ranges are dotted with lakes. The lakes are cold—usually too cold for swimming. The creeks and streams that carry water to them are often cloudy, almost milky. This is not pollution, but rock dust, created by glaciers grinding away at the mountains. When these minerals settle in the mountain lakes, the result is astonishing hues of blue and green. Some Wyomingites joke that their lakes look like toilet bowls filled with colored toilet cleaner. But these cloudy streams and brightly colored lakes actually contain some of the purest water in the United States.

WATER AND WEATHER

Between the mountain ranges are vast basins—bowl-like lowland areas. Water drains from the mountains and forms Wyoming's rivers. Some of these rivers spill into other rivers that eventually empty into the Pacific Ocean; others flow into a series of rivers leading to the Atlantic. The continental divide—the line separating water draining into the Atlantic from that headed for the Pacific—zigzags through western Wyoming's highlands.

The Great Divide Basin, in south-central Wyoming, does not drain at all. If much water accumulated there it would become an enormous lake. But the basin gets only a few inches of rain each

PREHISTORIC LIFE IN WYOMING

Few states can trace their natural history farther back in time than Wyoming. The state contains a treasure trove of fossils that allow scientists to construct a picture of life there going back millions of years, to a time before mountains—before, in fact, there was land in Wyoming at all.

Seventy-five million years ago, Wyoming was underneath a great sea that covered much of what is now the American West. As the sea shrank and grew, lush swamps and forests thrived on its edges, only to disappear again beneath the water. This process buried prehistoric life in layers of sediment that later hardened into rock, preserving fossils of Wyoming's earliest inhabitants. Scientists have recovered the remains of rhinoceroses, monkeys, crocodiles, cheetahs, and rabbit-sized horses in Wyoming. They have also found palm trees, roses, ferns, and many other ancestors of present-day plant life.

Most stunning, perhaps, are the dinosaur fossils that lie buried all across the state. Wyoming was once home to the triceratops, the stegosaurus, the huge brontosaurus, and the fierce tyrannosaurus rex.

Important fossils found in Wyoming are displayed in science museums everywhere. At Fossil Butte National Monument, near Kemmerer, visitors can even watch scientists dig them up.

year and is among the country's driest areas. It is one of the few places in the United States with desert sand dunes.

Several of Wyoming's rivers have carved majestic canyons. The Grand Canyon of the Yellowstone River is the most spectacular, with cliffs as high as 1,200 feet. The river cascades down two splendid waterfalls in Yellowstone Park. At the Lower Falls it plunges 308 feet (nearly twice as far as Niagara Falls in New York!).

When they are not streaming through canyons, Wyoming's creeks and rivers have a characteristic look to them: fast, shallow, and muddy. Their size changes dramatically with the seasons. In the spring and early summer, they are swollen with melted snow, but by late summer they can shrink to just a trickle or dry up altogether.

This is because Wyoming's climate is dry. The average yearly rainfall across the state is only thirteen inches. Still, parts of some mountain ranges get up to fifty inches a year. The dryness and high altitude also make most of the state cool in the summer. Yellowstone's average July temperature is only 59 degrees Fahrenheit, and back on the plains in Casper it is 71 degrees Fahrenheit. The summer weather doesn't last long. "If summer falls on a weekend," early settlers joked, "let's have a picnic."

The temperature falls below freezing every month of the year in the highlands. Over the course of the day the temperature changes a great deal. Nights are chilly, but afternoons are often warm. People learn to wear several layers of clothing, pulling them off as need be.

The long, frigid winters can seem to last forever. High winds and low temperatures produce dangerous windchill. Even a few minutes out of doors without proper clothing can lead to frostbite. Snow dusts the grasslands and western basins and dumps on the mountains. Some places in the Tetons and Yellowstone average 260 inches

The Grand Canyon of the Yellowstone River and its most awesome feature: the Lower Falls

Waterskiing, Wyoming style. Bitter winter weather doesn't keep Wyomingites from enjoying themselves outdoors.

of snowfall a year—almost 22 feet! Year-round, Wyoming is the second-coldest state in the nation; only Alaska is colder.

PLANTS AND ANIMALS

The incredible diversity of Wyoming's landscape has made it home to an equally diverse collection of plants and animals. Few states contain such a variety of wildlife: 119 species of mammals, 371 species of birds, and 9 species of snakes. The lakes and rivers contain a large assortment of fish, including salmon, bass, catfish, and seven kinds of trout. White pelicans and trumpeter swans soar over the lakes, as do peregrine falcons and ospreys.

Most of the nation's large mammals can be found in Wyoming. Moose and elk range across much of the state, living in the mountains by summer and foraging in the valleys by winter. The largest remaining herds of bighorn sheep live there, too. They descend from the Wind River Mountains to the foothills every winter to graze and mate. Everywhere, but especially on the eastern plains, white-tailed deer and the swift pronghorn antelope thrive.

Bighorn sheep once grazed Wyoming's mountainsides in vast numbers. Today few remain, so seeing one is a rare treat.

PRONGHORNS

If there were a footrace for all the animals in North America, the winner would be the pronghorn antelope, which hits speeds of more than sixty miles an hour. (At the Animal Olympics, it would win the silver medal—only the cheetah is faster.)

More pronghorns live in Wyoming than anywhere else. They are timid creatures that usually move in groups, employing a "safety in numbers" approach to survival. Yet pronghorns have few fearsome predators in Wyoming (apart from people). Why are they so fast and so cautious? One zoologist, John A. Byers, thinks that pronghorns developed these traits millions of years ago, when cheetahs, lions, and hyenas lived in Wyoming and preyed on the pronghorn. The last of these predators left the area about ten thousand years ago, but today's pronghorns act as though they were still present. It's as if the antelopes are "living with the ghosts" of their ancient enemies, Dr. Byers says.

The federal government owns almost half the land in Wyoming, including Grand Teton and Yellowstone National Parks, five national forests, and several wildlife refuges. These offer animals and plants places to live where human development poses little threat. The Thunder Basin National Grassland in northeastern Wyoming helps preserve the over 150 kinds of grass that are native to the state. The national forests sustain towering ponderosa and lodgepole pines and Douglas firs, and an environment friendly to creatures like squirrels, raccoons, pocket gophers, weasels, and wildcats. In several protected locations, a few dozen of the world's last black-footed ferrets are struggling to rebuild their numbers. They are the most endangered mammal in North America.

Seventy-five million bison once lived in the American West, but

Bison were slaughtered by the millions in the late nineteenth century. The largest remaining herds live in Wyoming.

they were hunted nearly to extinction in the nineteenth century. By 1905, a single ragged herd of twenty-five bison remained in Yellowstone Park. Today the Yellowstone bison herd numbers several thousand—the largest in the world. But they are still in danger, for some carry brucellosis, a disease that can spread to cattle. When bison wander out of Yellowstone into Montana, that state has them slaughtered to protect its cattle industry. During the severe winter of 1997, many bison could not find enough food in Yellowstone. Some died of starvation; others headed for Montana to find grass and were killed. It may take many years for the herd to recover from that cruel winter.

LIVING WITH WILDLIFE

Laws protecting the state's animals and environment are support-ed by many Wyomingites. But ranchers and mining companies often oppose environmental programs that could limit their prof-its or their use of publicly owned land. In the past, they usually got their way. Early in the century, ranchers convinced the govern-ment to pay hunters to slaughter wolves that occasionally preyed on their livestock. By the 1920s, the last of Wyoming's wolf packs had been exterminated.

In the early 1990s, environmentalists proposed a plan to rein-troduce wolves to Yellowstone National Park. Most ranchers fiercely opposed this idea, fearing that the wolves would leave the park to dine on their cattle and sheep. They came to public meetings car-rying signs reading WYOMING IS NOT A ZOO and WOLVES DON'T PAY TAXES. But others supported the wolves' return just as fiercely. "I

Since the gray wolf's return to Yellowstone, the population of rodents and small mammals has jumped. Scientists say this is because the wolves prey on coyotes, which had nearly wiped out some species during the wolves' long absence from the park.

know what it means to be an animal who doesn't know where to go, like the wolf and the grizzly bear," said Bill Tallbull, a Cheyenne Indian. "Now, I live on the reservation. It's my sanctuary. Let's let Yellowstone National Park be the sanctuary for the wolf."

Scientists predicted that the wolves would kill little livestock, and environmental organizations promised to pay ranchers if they did. Finally, the project was approved. In 1995, three wolf packs

LAND AND WATER

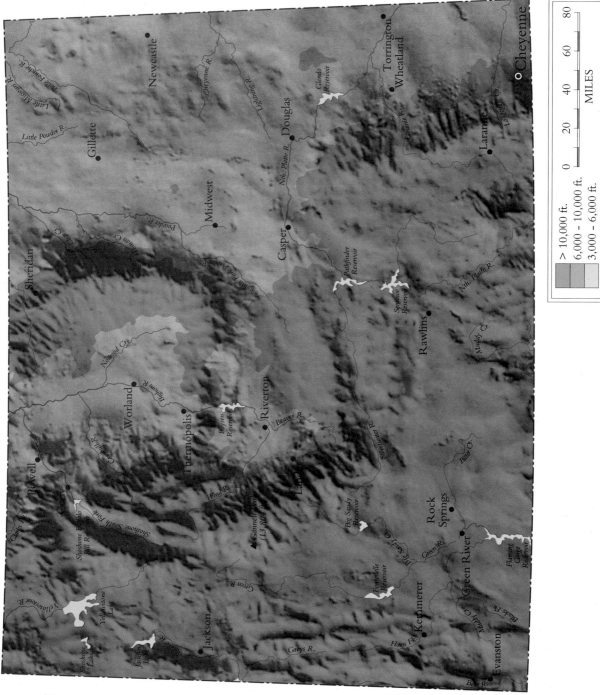

were captured in Canada and released in Yellowstone. Both sides of the conflict have followed the wolves' every move since then. Fortunately, the wolves are more interested in raising pups than in killing sheep. Their numbers are growing rapidly, and half of Wyomingites now support their return.

A big advantage for Wyoming's wildlife is that the state's human population is tiny. Only about 490,000 people live in Wyoming, making it the least populated state in the country. That is an average of only five people per square mile (compared to an average of sixty-seven people per square mile for the whole United States).

Many Wyoming towns were originally built along major transportation routes. Casper grew up on the site of a military fort along the Oregon Trail, and Cheyenne is one of several towns that sprung up when the nation's first transcontinental railroad was built across southern Wyoming in 1868. Sheridan and Gillette, the major towns in the northeast, sprouted up around the cattle business and the rich oil and coal deposits in the area. And towns like Cody and Jackson grew around tourist attractions: they are the gateways to Yellowstone and Grand Teton National Parks.

Not all cities were lucky enough to develop near important resources. Wyoming is scattered with ghost towns—communities that died out because there was little opportunity to prosper there. In such places as Encampment, the sun beats down on rotting boards, and grass grows over the road. Abandoned buildings become homes for wild animals. Slowly, the traces of settlement are swallowed up by the landscape, and once again the towering mountains and wide, empty spaces take over.

2 HIGH COUNTRY HISTORY

Island Lake, Wind River Range, by Albert Bierstadt

People have lived in what is now Wyoming for more than ten thousand years. The first Wyomingites moved frequently in search of food. They ate roots, seeds, and small animals. Wyoming was warmer and wetter then. As it dried up and cooled down, hunting and gathering became more difficult, and these earliest inhabitants disappeared.

NATIVE AMERICAN LIFE

The next humans arrived in Wyoming several thousand years later, probably following herds of grazing animals. These ancestors of modern Indians invented the bow and arrow to improve their hunting. Families and small bands cooperated on hunts of bison, deer, and other animals.

Slowly, these groups joined together to become large tribes with common cultures. Wyoming's Indians lived in tepees made of buffalo hides, which could be easily dismantled and transported as they followed the buffalo herds and other game that they depended on for survival.

By the time Europeans arrived in the Americas five hundred years ago, several tribes were living at least part of the time in Wyoming. The largest groups were the Shoshones and the Arapahos. But the

According to Alfred Jacob Miller, who painted this picture, at the beginning of a buffalo hunt, the Indians "all start at once with frightful yells and commence racing around the herd."

Lakotas, Crows, Cheyennes, Bannocks, Blackfeet, and Northern Utes also ranged into what would become Wyoming.

OUTSIDERS ARRIVE

Nobody knows when the first European entered Wyoming. Between 1804 and 1806, the first U.S. expedition through the area, led by Meriwether Lewis and William Clark, crossed the continent to the Pacific Ocean, but passed north of Wyoming. One of its members, John Colter, left the expedition as it returned east to scout the Yellowstone and Teton areas. Although other Europeans may have come before him, Colter was the first to tell about the area.

Colter's stories brought more explorers to Wyoming. Fur trappers soon joined the explorers. Then came fur traders, who exchanged supplies and money for pelts. For the most part, Indians had good relations with these "mountain men." They exchanged pelts for guns, compasses, and other tools. Some Indians married fur traders, and each group benefited from the other's knowledge.

Meanwhile, a growing number of Americans began making the long cross-country journey to settle in Oregon and California. The fur traders had explored possible routes to the West and knew that there were very few places where a wagon could cross the Rockies. The best gap in the long wall of mountains was at South Pass in southwest Wyoming.

That is how the Oregon Trail, the most important path to the Far West, came to cross Wyoming. Travelers entered the future state at Fort Laramie, the last place to buy supplies before crossing the mountains. Weeks later, as the once-distant peaks grew closer, they would camp in the shadows of a great rock rising from the plains called Independence Rock. Many travelers carved their names and the date into the granite there. This early graffiti assured friends and family who followed that they had continued west and were safe.

Each year the traffic increased. Mormons began using the trail to reach the religious community they were building at Salt Lake City, Utah. Gold was discovered in California in 1849, and traffic

Fort Laramie was one of the most important stops on the Oregon Trail as traffic grew during the 1840s.

on the trail mushroomed. Before the flow stopped, a quarter of a million travelers had made the journey. The deep ruts cut by their wagons can still be seen in many places 150 years later.

WAR BETWEEN INDIANS AND SETTLERS

Few of the early travelers on the Oregon Trail stayed in Wyoming (unless you count the bodies of those who died during the brutal journey). Nevertheless, they upset the way of life of the Indians who lived there. Travelers drove away the wildlife the Indians depended on for food. And now newcomers began settling in Wyoming, particularly traders, gold prospectors, and the soldiers sent to protect them.

In the 1860s, tensions between whites and Indians boiled over in the country surrounding the Oregon Trail. Army massacres of Indians in northern Colorado and southern Idaho killed hundreds of people. Indians struck back in a series of attacks on soldiers and settlers, stopping traffic on the Oregon Trail. In 1866, a group of Lakota Indians, led by Chief Red Cloud, surprised a group of U.S. cavalry near Fort Kearney in northern Wyoming and killed all eighty-one of them in a bloody fight. After two more years of smaller battles, a treaty signed in 1868 at Fort Laramie ended the war. The

The Oregon Trail was littered with tools, furniture, even pianos abandoned by migrants when they confronted the cruel mountain passes.

Lakota chief Red Cloud. In 1868, the United States "made a treaty with Red Cloud that said our country would be ours as long as grass should grow and water flow," remembered holy man Black Elk. "You can see that it is not the grass and the water that have forgotten."

Indians agreed to allow roads and railroads to be built, and the U.S. government promised to set aside a large reservation for Indians in what is now western South Dakota and to keep new settlers from going there.

A RAILROAD CREATES A TERRITORY

In the half-century before the Fort Laramie Treaty of 1868, the newcomers from the East had transformed life in Wyoming. But the events of the next few years made all those changes seem small.

The Union Pacific Railroad, built across southern Wyoming beginning in 1867, changed life in Wyoming forever.

The reason was the coming of the railroad. The U.S. government wanted trains to replace wagon travel on slow, hazardous roads like the Oregon Trail. The rail route had to be fairly flat, and it had to be close to coal and water to fuel the steam locomotives that pulled the trains. The Union Pacific Railroad chose a route across southern Wyoming that had all of these advantages.

Fur trappers had brought trading posts to Wyoming, and the Oregon Trail had brought military forts, but the railroad brought cities. Cheyenne, Laramie, Rawlins, Rock Springs, Green River, and Evanston all grew up overnight along the rails. At first these places

THE ROCK SPRINGS MASSACRE

The Union Pacific Railroad employed many Wyomingites in the coal mines it operated to fuel its trains. The miners' lives were harsh, and the pay was poor. In 1875, the miners went on strike. The Union Pacific fired them and replaced them with workers from China.

Chinese laborers had done much of the hard work to build the railroad in the first place. They were willing to work for the railroad's low wages and they did not join the miners' labor unions. The other workers blamed the Chinese for their failed strike and the pitiful wages they continued to earn.

By 1885, 331 Chinese worked with 150 whites in the coal mines near Rock Springs. One day a fight broke out that turned into a riot. Fueled by racial prejudice, the crowd killed 28 Chinese workers and injured 15 others. Hundreds of Chinese were driven out of town, and their homes were set on fire.

Sixteen men were arrested for participating in the Rock Springs Massacre, but none were ever brought to trial because a grand jury refused to charge them. Governor Francis E. Warren called the massacre "the most damnable and brutal outrage that ever occurred in any country," but few other Wyomingites sympathized with the Chinese. After the massacre, most of them left Wyoming.

looked more like campgrounds than permanent towns—most of the first "buildings" were actually tents. People streamed in from the East to fill them—some coming to work on the railroad, others to open businesses and buy the best land. Still others were prospectors searching for gold. They found a little near South Pass, which lured a new wave of fortune-seekers into the area. They also discovered a lot of coal, which could be mined to fuel the trains.

In 1868, Wyoming became a territory. When its first legislature met in 1869, one of its first laws gave women the right to vote. Nowhere else in the world did women have this liberty. Women's rights leader Susan B. Anthony declared, "Wyoming is the first place on God's green earth which could consistently claim to be the land of the free."

One reason Wyoming gave women the right to vote was because it was eager to attract more people from the East—especially women. In 1870, six out of seven settlers were men, and many of them were lonely. However, few new settlers came to Wyoming until gold was discovered in the Black Hills near the Dakota-Wyoming border. By 1875, thousands of prospectors were invading the Indian reservation established by the Fort Laramie Treaty just seven years earlier.

The U.S. government could do little to keep prospectors away from this Indian land, and a new war broke out. In November 1876, Colonel R. S. MacKenzie destroyed a Cheyenne Indian encampment along the Powder River. Deprived of food and shelter, many Indians froze or starved to death. The survivors fled to Montana or surrendered and agreed to live on much smaller reservations. The Indians had lost control of the plains forever.

HOME ON THE RANGE

With most Indians forced from their lands, Wyoming entered a new era. The vast rangelands were perfect for raising cattle, and the Union Pacific Railroad was perfect for transporting them to

THE EQUALITY STATE

Wyoming is called the Equality State because it was the first place to grant women the right to vote. Wyoming women have achieved a remarkable number of other political "firsts":

Esther Morris was appointed the world's first female justice of the peace in 1870 in South Pass City.

Eliza Stewart became the first woman ever to serve on a jury in 1870. This was such a big event that King Wilhelm I of Prussia sent a telegram to President Ulysses S. Grant congratulating him.

Estelle Reel was elected Wyoming's superintendent of education in 1894, making her the first woman to win a statewide election in the United States.

Susan Wissler became Wyoming's first female mayor in 1911, even though she declared she didn't want the job. The townspeople of Douglas ignored that and elected her anyway! She was re-elected twice.

In 1920, the town of Jackson elected the country's first all-woman government.

And in 1924, Nellie Tayloe Ross became the first female governor in the United States.

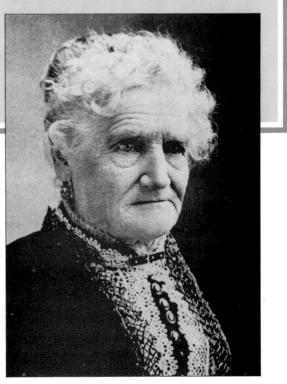

Esther Morris

The Indians of the Great Plains often used a travois, which was dragged behind a horse or dog, to move from one place to another.

market in the cities back east. The age of the cowboy had begun.

In just a few years, cattle ranches sprouted up all over Wyoming's eastern plains. The state's population increased as more easterners arrived, eager to own ranches or to work as cowboys.

Soon the rangeland was actually crowded. In some places the grass could not grow back as rapidly as the cattle swallowed it. During the hard winter of 1886–1887, disaster struck. The weather was so cold, and the snow so deep, that cattle could not find water and food. Hundreds of thousands of them died. The cattle business did not go bust, but its boom years were over.

LAW AND DISORDER

Twenty years after Wyoming became a territory, its population had climbed to over 60,000. Many clamored for Congress to grant Wyoming full statehood. They got their wish on July 10, 1890, when Wyoming became the nation's forty-fourth state.

The new state was now responsible for its own law and order, but this was not easy. For years, rustlers had been stealing cattle from the open rangelands. Now the cattle barons who owned the largest ranches accused smaller ranchers of this crime. In 1892, a group of Texas gunmen hired by the big ranchers killed two suspected rustlers in Johnson County. Their neighbors armed themselves and surrounded the Texans, who had holed up at a nearby ranch. The neighbors were preparing to blow up the ranch when U.S. soldiers arrived to rescue the gunmen. Wyomingites like journalist Asa Mercer were outraged: "The invasion," he wrote, "was the crowning infamy of the ages." A solo outlaw, Tom Horn, also made his living as a killer hired to terrify small ranchers. To show that he was the one who had carried out the job, Horn always put a rock under the head of his victim. Horn was finally captured and hung in 1903.

Wyoming's rangelands were just as good for raising sheep as cattle, and sheep ranches began competing for space on the plains. Cattle ranchers pressured the sheepherders to stay out of areas they used to graze cattle. Sheep ranchers pointed out that the open range was owned by the government and that everyone had an equal right to use it. For years, the cattle barons' masked gunmen harassed the sheep ranches, shooting or dynamiting herds of sheep—and sometimes killing sheepherders. Finally, seven cattle-

GOOD-BYE, OLD PAINT

The cowboy—the sentimental cowboy—sang this sad farewell song at the end of a rare evening in town. It was the last waltz, and as he saddled up Old Paint and headed back to the lonesome ranch, he never knew if there would be a next time.

Good - bye, old paint, I'm a - leav - ing Chey - enne. Good -

bye, old paint, I'm a - leav - ing Chey - enne.

Fine

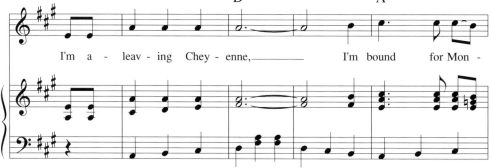

Verse

I'm a - leav - ing Chey - enne,_____ I'm bound for Mon -

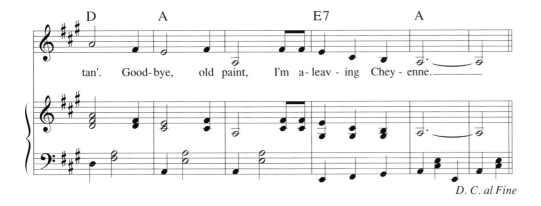

tan'. Good-bye,   old paint,   I'm a-leav-ing Chey-enne.

D. C. al Fine

In the 1870s and 1880s cowboy life reached its heyday. But harsh winters and falling beef prices soon changed conditions on the range.

Sheep ranching actually surpassed cattle ranching in value early in the twentieth century. The rivalry between cattle and sheep ranchers still simmers today in Wyoming.

men were arrested in 1909 for killing sheep ranchers near the town of Ten Sleep. Five of them went to jail, and the violence largely ended. Even today, though, cattle and sheep ranchers are not the best of friends.

INTO THE TWENTIETH CENTURY

Wyoming's population more than doubled during the first twenty years after statehood. Coal mining and oil drilling boomed. By

1914, the state was producing six million barrels of crude oil every year for America's growing fleet of automobiles. That amount doubled during World War I, as Wyoming supplied fuel, food, and soldiers to the nation's war effort.

But wartime prosperity did not last long. The Great Depression, which rocked America during the 1930s, began much earlier in Wyoming. The state's livestock, coal, and oil industries all suffered from falling prices during the 1920s. Farmers and ranchers endured droughts, coal producers were shut down by strikes, and the oil

In the early twentieth century, oil wells sprang up all over Wyoming.

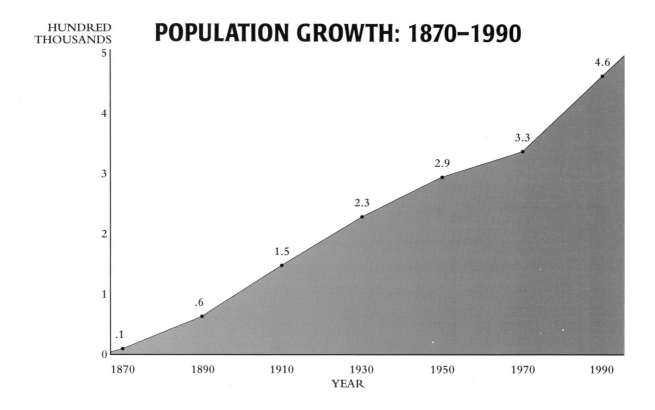

POPULATION GROWTH: 1870–1990

HUNDRED
THOUSANDS

YEAR

industry faced stiff competition from other states. Since these industries made up most of Wyoming's economy, the whole state was troubled. More than half the state's banks closed during the 1920s, costing some Wyomingites all their savings—a calamity the rest of the country would face a decade later.

The one bright spot was the rise in tourism. Americans in more prosperous states began discovering the natural beauty of Wyoming, and by the 1920s automobiles could take them there. Dude ranches, which gave tourists a taste of the cowboy's life, flourished.

When the nationwide depression hit in the early 1930s, Wyoming's hard times got worse. By 1933, 20,000 Wyomingites were unemployed, and Wyoming relied more than almost any other state on government assistance. Even cattle ranchers, whose land and livestock were once worth millions of dollars, received federal money to keep them from going out of business.

THE MODERN WORLD

When the United States entered World War II in 1941, Wyoming again contributed raw materials to the war effort, particularly oil, coal, and beef. Near Douglas, a prisoner-of-war camp was built, which soon filled with Italian and German prisoners.

Farther west, at Heart Mountain, another kind of camp was built—this one to hold Americans. The U.S. government had decided to confine Japanese Americans in internment camps because it feared they would cooperate with Japan, an enemy country during the war. Although there was practically no evidence that this was true, almost 11,000 Japanese Americans, mostly from California, wound up at Heart Mountain. They lived in rows of dreary tar paper barracks surrounded by barbed wire. Many lost their homes and businesses during their confinement. Despite this injustice, most Wyomingites were unsympathetic. "We do not want a single one of these evacuees to remain in Wyoming," declared Governor Lester C. Hunt. He needn't have worried; when they were freed, nearly all left Wyoming as quickly as they could. In 1988, Congress paid money to the victims of this misguided wartime policy and issued an apology.

When World War II ended in 1945, prosperity returned to Wyoming and the rest of the country. The war had defeated the Great Depression, and the state's beef and minerals brought good prices again. Coal and oil replaced cattle as Wyoming's most important products. Wyoming's large deposits of uranium, used to run nuclear power plants and to make nuclear weapons, also contributed to the state's postwar boom.

Uranium mining was a boom industry after World War II, but prices for the mineral fell in the 1980s, leaving many workers without a job.

But in the 1980s, oil, coal, and uranium prices tumbled, and many young workers moved out of the state in search of work. "Rather than choose Wyoming's way," says Paul Krza, a Wyomingite who moved to Colorado, "many residents, especially the young, choose the highway." Today, energy prices are up, and the economy is doing better—but only time will tell whether Wyoming can develop new reasons for residents to stay, work, and help their state prosper.

3 SHARING THE RICHES

The state capitol in Cheyenne

As the Union Pacific blazed its trail across southern Wyoming in 1868, boomtowns like Cheyenne and Laramie filled with rowdy railroad workers and enough outlaws and desperadoes to make life miserable and dangerous. Citizens often took the law into their own hands, but their vigilante justice was seldom fair. "We're going to give you a fair trial," their victims were promised, "followed by a first-class hanging." It took the establishment of a state government in Wyoming to create true law and order, settle disputes honestly, and coordinate the projects that have made the state a good place to live.

INSIDE GOVERNMENT

Wyoming's government is based on the state constitution, which was written in 1889. The constitution can be changed only if two-thirds of the state legislature and a majority of the state's voters approve. Wyoming's constitution calls for three branches of government: executive, legislative, and judicial.

Executive. The executive branch is headed by the governor, who is elected every four years. The governor makes recommendations about which laws the state legislature should pass. Governors can veto laws they don't like, and unless two-thirds of the legislators vote to override a veto, the governor has the final say. Working

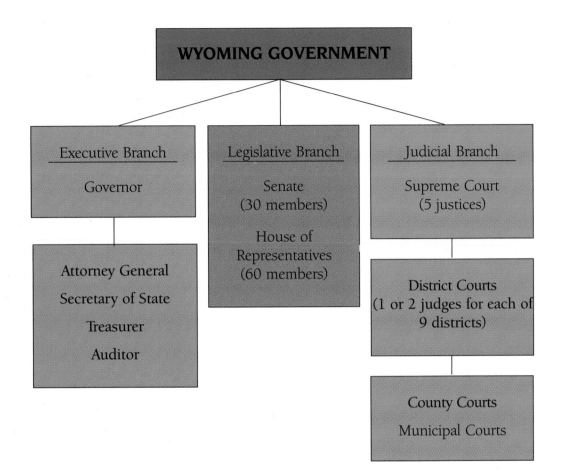

WYOMING GOVERNMENT

Executive Branch

Governor

Attorney General

Secretary of State

Treasurer

Auditor

Legislative Branch

Senate
(30 members)

House of
Representatives
(60 members)

Judicial Branch

Supreme Court
(5 justices)

District Courts
(1 or 2 judges for each of
9 districts)

County Courts

Municipal Courts

under the governor are other executive officials, like the secretary of state, the attorney general, and the state treasurer. These officials, and the departments they lead, work out the details of *executing* the laws—making sure, for example, that Wyoming's schools receive the correct amount of money.

Legislative. The legislative branch consists of a house of representatives and a senate. The house has sixty members who are elected to two-year terms; the thirty senators are elected to four-year terms. All new laws (and changes to old ones) are proposed, discussed, and voted on by these legislators. The legislature meets every January, and its meetings cannot last for more than forty days. This is shorter than the legislative sessions of most states and reflects Wyomingites' wish to restrict government activity.

Judicial. At the top of the judicial branch is a supreme court with five justices. They are appointed by the governor and serve eight-year terms. The supreme court sometimes clarifies the meaning of vaguely worded laws and decides whether laws violate the state constitution. Wyoming also has nine judicial districts, each with one or two judges, who are appointed by the governor to six-year terms. These courts handle civil and criminal trials and appeals of verdicts reached by county and municipal courts.

COWBOY POLITICS

Typically, Wyomingites are conservative. They believe that government should be small and its powers should be limited. They think that the federal government is too powerful and wish it had a smaller role in Wyoming. Since the beginning, most Wyoming voters and elected officials have been Republicans. Today, Wyoming is one of the most Republican states in the country. Wyomingites prefer a lot of freedom to determine how they live. Most oppose laws making it hard to own a gun, for example. As former senator Alan Simpson puts it, "In the Cowboy State, gun control simply means how steady you hold your rifle."

Most Wyomingites agree that taxes should be low. Wyoming is one of the few states that has no income tax, which means it has less money to fund government programs than most other states. A special tax on minerals mined in the state makes up some of the

"Cowboys are just like a pile of rocks," writes rancher Gretel Ehrlich. "They get climbed on, kicked, rained and snowed on, scuffed up by the wind. Their job is 'just to take it.'"

difference. The state has to raise money to pay for everything from building roads and maintaining public schools to managing wildlife and providing assistance to the poor. Still, Wyoming spends more than the national average for police and crime prevention and has one of the lowest crime rates in the country.

Wyoming also spends a lot on education—more money per pupil than any state but Alaska. This is partly because a high proportion of its people are schoolchildren (Wyoming has one of the youngest populations in the country). Another reason is that the population is spread thinly across a lot of space, so the state must run many small schools in remote locations. Willow Creek School, for example, is twenty-five miles from the nearest town. It has only five students, but the state pays for an aide as well as the teacher, Kari Docktor. The school even includes an apartment for Docktor. "Even though I have a four-wheel-drive truck," she explains, "I can't live in town; I'd miss school whenever the weather got bad or I had a breakdown. I've had a dozen flat tires this year already!"

Wyoming's tiny communities, like Kelly, near Jackson Hole, make for small schools.

PROUD TO BE A TARGET

Just outside Cheyenne is Warren Air Force Base, the site of most of the nation's intercontinental ballistic missiles (ICBMs). These weapons can be launched from underground silos and rocket halfway around the world before releasing nuclear warheads capable of destroying a whole city. After World War II, the United States and the Soviet Union built thousands of ICBMs and pointed them at each other in what was called the cold war. Everyone figured that a Soviet attack would attempt to destroy as many American missiles as possible. Yet, when America's first ICBMs came to Warren in 1958, the mayor of Cheyenne declared, "Cheyenne is proud to be the nation's number one target for enemy missiles."

The United States put the missiles in Cheyenne partly because it was easy to build deep silos there to protect them from attack. But it was also a political decision. Wyoming was among the nation's most conservative states, strongly in favor of the military. And the city valued the jobs and money that came from having a military base next door. Few cities would have been as "proud to be a target" as Cheyenne.

Some people have always protested the missiles. Now that the cold war is over, opposition seems to be growing. "We have to make people aware that the missiles are still in the ground and are still dangerous," says Margaret Laybourn, who has been protesting since the first ICBM arrived.

Wyoming produces the most coal of any state in the nation.

Such schools are obviously more expensive per pupil than big-city schools. However, Willow Creek's students get a lot of attention and score high on math and reading tests—like the rest of Wyoming's kids.

Health care can be a worry for Wyomingites because many of the smallest towns have no hospitals or doctors close by. The state does what it can to encourage doctors to practice in Wyoming, but it faces the same problem with health care that it does with schools: there aren't enough people in many areas to support a doctor's office, let alone a hospital. It is sometimes necessary to travel great distances for help with a difficult medical problem. In 1997, for example, nine-year-old Eman Khan of Sheridan needed a heart

transplant, but her hospital was four hundred miles away in Denver, Colorado. When a heart became available, she had only three hours to get to Denver. Her parents could not find a pilot to fly her there in time, so the heart went to someone else.

THE ENERGY STATE

Although Wyoming has long been associated with cattle ranching, today energy is its most important industry. Rigs for drilling oil and gas bob along roadsides across the state. Wyoming produces more coal than any other state. "We fill up eight or nine trains, each a mile long, every day," says Ken Miller of the Black Thunder coal

GROSS STATE PRODUCT: $19.5 BILLION

(2000 estimated)

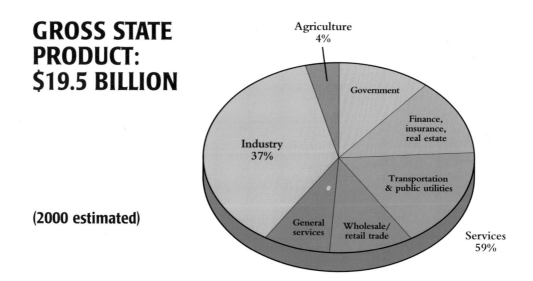

Agriculture 4%

Government

Finance, insurance, real estate

Industry 37%

Transportation & public utilities

General services

Wholesale/ retail trade

Services 59%

mine in the Powder River Basin. Some of this coal fuels the giant Jim Bridger power plant near Rock Springs. The plant towers twenty-four stories above the sandy flatlands of the Great Divide Basin, which easily makes it the tallest building in Wyoming. It generates four times more electricity than Wyoming can use. Most of the rest is sold to other states.

The names of two other minerals mined in Wyoming are unknown to most Americans, even though they use them almost every day. One is trona (also called soda ash), and Wyoming has almost the world's entire natural supply at a single giant mine near the town of Green River. Trona is an ingredient in glass, paper, and baking soda and is also used in making iron and steel. (This book probably contains traces of Wyoming trona. Look out the window and you are probably looking through Wyoming.)

The other unfamiliar mineral important to Wyoming's economy is bentonite—a fancy name for a fancy kind of mud. Bentonite can

EARNING A LIVING

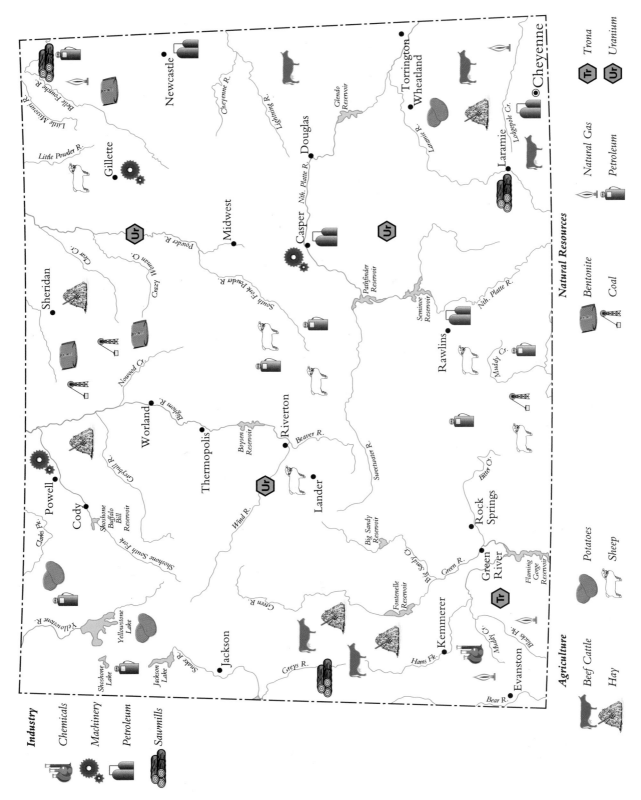

Industry

Chemicals

Machinery

Petroleum

Sawmills

Agriculture

Beef Cattle

Hay

Potatoes

Sheep

Natural Resources

Trona

Uranium

Natural Gas

Petroleum

Bentonite

Coal

absorb fifteen times its volume in water, and when wet it becomes so slippery that cars can barely drive over it. But Wyoming is lucky to have large deposits of bentonite, for it is used in making glue, paint, detergent, and polish, not to mention makeup, toothpaste, and cat litter.

Vast Wyoming, with so few people and cities, also has few farms. This is mostly because the state receives little rainfall. Farms are mainly located in the eastern part of the state. They grow beans, sugar beets, and potatoes. They also raise grain and hay to feed livestock. The most successful farms use irrigation systems to bring a steady supply of water to the crops.

What Wyoming lacks in farms it makes up for in ranches, which occupy 96 percent of its agricultural land. For some ranchers, Wyoming's mythic cowboy lifestyle seems almost real. Thomas McNamee loves "the beautiful horses, the beautiful leather, the sun-crinkled squint toward the distant horizon." But he adds, this life also involves "long hours, poor money, guaranteed uncertainty, and unending, brutally hard work." Fewer Wyoming ranches raise sheep today, but the beef industry is still strong, and the cowboy on the Wyoming license plate remains a good symbol for the state's economy.

AN ECONOMY AT A CROSSROADS

Wyoming is fortunate to have rich natural resources. But relying on them for its economic well-being is risky. Agricultural and mineral prices rise and fall, and the state's economy rises and falls with them. When prices are high, there are plenty of jobs. When prices

Although the days of vast cattle drives are long gone, ranching is still a major industry in Wyoming.

plummet, jobs disappear—and people disappear, too. The strongest days of Wyoming's economy, when oil, gas, coal, and uranium prices were especially high, are over—at least for now. Still, the state's economy is growing, and people are arriving from other states in search of work.

Wyoming's growth has been slower than that of neighboring

states, though, because its economy is so dependent on industries like coal and oil. Wyoming never developed large cities with the services and professional experts needed to support a mix of other industries. Only about ten thousand Wyomingites have jobs in manufacturing—easily the smallest factory workforce in the country. Wyoming also has few jobs in fields like banking or computing. Because the state has few high-paying, high-skill jobs, the average Wyoming worker makes about four thousand dollars less than the national average each year.

Even so, poverty is relatively low. Most of Wyoming's poor are concentrated in small towns or rural areas where there are few jobs. The worst poverty is on the Wind River Indian Reservation. Indians receive some money from mining on the reservation, but jobs are scarce, and unemployment is extremely high. Many families make do only because reservation communities are generous. Neighbors share as much as they can—but they are unlikely to have many resources, either.

Wyoming's government is trying to improve such economic trouble spots by attracting businesses, but it's not easy. "We don't have a lot of existing buildings or industrial parks," notes George Gault of the Wyoming State Division of Economic and Community Development. "We don't have a major supply of skilled, trained employees for high-tech business . . . it's just a little too far from the mainstream." Wyoming has tried to attract manufacturers by holding down taxes and advertising the state's low wages. "Wyoming is the cheapest place in the country to do business," boosters claim. So far, though, these efforts have not been very successful.

Perhaps the brightest spot in today's economy is Wyoming's

Poverty remains the biggest problem for Wyoming's Indians; few economic opportunities exist where most Indians live.

third-largest industry—tourism. About seven million people visit Wyoming every year (fifteen times the state's population!). Tourism provides jobs to a variety of workers: ski patrols, motel operators, park rangers, restaurant workers, and tour guides. The problem with many of these jobs is that they are seasonal—they disappear

Tourism may be the future of Wyoming's economy, as this park ranger, and others who cater to the state's growing number of visitors, can confirm.

when the tourist season ends. Unemployment therefore remains a seasonal problem for tourism workers as well.

Wyoming's economy is at a crossroads, and state residents argue about which direction it should go. Some say Wyoming should continue to rely on mining. Others say Wyoming should build a mixed economy that can withstand the boom and bust of changing mineral prices, while also preserving the environment in order to attract tourists and new residents. Neither of these paths will be easy to travel, but Wyomingites' long tradition of hard work and self-reliance should help them meet their economic challenges.

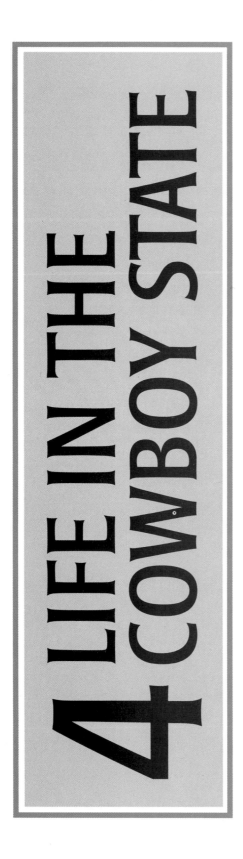

4 LIFE IN THE COWBOY STATE

Living in Wyoming is different from living in any other state. "It's not dull, not humdrum, not 'average,'" claims Nathaniel Burt, who lives in Jackson Hole. There are so few people, and so much room. Wyomingites balance these two facts in remarkable ways. They celebrate the land by working and playing close to it, and they cherish each other, striving to keep far-flung communities together.

CITIES AND TOWNS

Contrary to what outsiders think, the typical Wyomingite doesn't live in a rustic cabin in the wilderness. For most, home is in a city or town. Life in Wyoming's larger cities is a lot like city life in other parts of the country. Neighborhoods in Casper and Cheyenne would not look out of place in most other cities of the same size. Kids attend schools and hang out at shopping malls that could be anywhere.

Smaller towns are more likely to fit the image of rugged, historic Wyoming. Towns like Buffalo, home to 3,400 people on the northeastern plains, have preserved the flavor of life from half a century ago or more. Buffalo's Main Street is lined with old brick buildings. Faded signs still adorn their sides, showing that they were once hotels and banks. Now, however, they are more likely to be art galleries, antique shops, and restaurants.

Some Wyoming towns are little more than a mishmash of gas stations, fast food restaurants, and mobile homes spreading from the old town center. Even those who really love these towns admit that they are not beautiful. But they are often busy places, home to many unmarried workers and young families.

Regardless of their individual characters, Wyoming towns are outposts on the land, the focus of attention for miles around. They are where families go to see their neighbors, where children meet for school. For rural Wyomingites, "going to town" may mean

TEN LARGEST CITIES

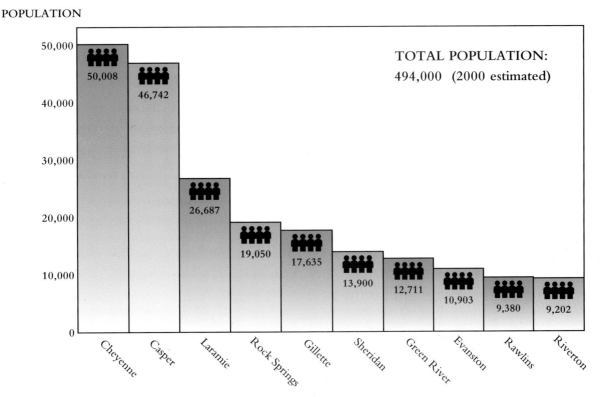

POPULATION

TOTAL POPULATION:
494,000 (2000 estimated)

50,000 — 50,008
46,742
40,000
30,000
26,687
20,000 — 19,050
17,635
13,900
12,711
10,000 — 10,903
9,380   9,202
0

Cheyenne · Casper · Laramie · Rock Springs · Gillette · Sheridan · Green River · Evanston · Rawlins · Riverton

visiting a community of only several hundred people with a grocery store, a place to rent videos, and churches, bars, and restaurants where people can gather. For Nate Buckingham, a kid who lives outside of Kaycee, Wyoming, town is also a place to skateboard—the ranch where he lives is twenty-five miles from the nearest pavement!

Wyomingites cherish the elbowroom their remote towns and ranches provide them. This is why the automobile is such an important part of life in Wyoming. Forget about horses—Wyoming has the highest rate of motor vehicle ownership in the country. (To go with this, it also has one of the highest rates of traffic deaths.)

THROUGH THE SEASONS

Many towns plan festivals and events for the winter months. The International Rocky Mountain Stage Stop Sled Dog Race takes place over more than a week on a four-hundred-mile course that visits towns in Wyoming's southwestern corner. The towns are resting points at the end of each race day, and the arrival of the exhausted sledders and their dogs sparks a celebration each night. In tiny Alpine, three hundred tickets are sold for the banquet to welcome the racers (several times more than the population of the entire town). While the sled drivers eat with the townspeople, the dogs wolf down concoctions of beef, chicken, fish, and vitamins to restore their strength for the next day's racing.

Even with such lively events, Wyoming winters can be long and lonely. Hundreds of miles of roads are routinely closed all winter because of snow. Many more miles of roads get shut down

"Over a 400-mile race, I run 20 miles a day," says dogsledder Billy Snodgrass of Dubois, who packs plenty of snacks when he competes. When a moose threatened his team, "I threw a block of frozen orange juice at her."

ETHNIC WYOMING

African
American

American Indian,
Inuit, Aleutian

Other

Asian,
Pacific Islander

Hispanic

White

temporarily when snowstorms and wind make them impassable—
even Wyoming's two interstate highways, its major ties to the
outside world.

But winter weather is more an adventure than a disaster for
Wyomingites. It makes the state one of the nation's finest spots
for skiing and snowmobiling. Serious skiers consider the Jackson
Hole Ski Resort among the best in the world, and even beginners,
gazing across the valley at the Teton Range, can tell that it is one
of the most beautiful. Snowmobiling is even more popular than
skiing. Wyoming has a large network of snowmobile trails, many
reaching wild areas far from the nearest roads. A common road-
side scene in the winter is rows of four-wheel-drive trucks parked at
trailheads. The empty snowmobile trailers behind them show how
many groups are out gunning through the thick snowdrifts on their

KIDS AND CARS

Wyoming is a state of great distances. Some children ride the bus seventy-five miles each way to school. They can finish all their homework before they get home!

Wyoming allows fourteen-year-olds to get a driver's license if they need it to get to school. On private land, children can drive at any age. Brent Buckingham, a fifth grader, sometimes drives an old blue pickup truck to help his father herd sheep on the Willow Creek Ranch near Kaycee.

Even though there's no traffic, it's not always easy. One frigid morning, Brent drove the pickup while his father stood in back, throwing sacks of corn to the sheep. "When I came to the place where the ground starts to slope down I turned to avoid a canyon . . . and the truck started to point down and speed up a lot. I froze up like a board," the eleven-year-old recalls. "The truck was aimed for a little group of sheep who had their heads down . . . when the truck got to the little herd I heard a 'ka-thunk!'" Brent felt horrible. "The worst part of it was to think that I actually ran over a sheep and broke another's leg. . . . Mom thought it was funny, but I didn't. Dad talked it over with me and I am slowly getting over it, but I still don't like to think about it much."

sleds. Some accuse these "belt-heads" of disturbing wildlife, which have a hard enough time as it is searching for food in the deep snow. "That's nonsense," one sledder claims. "Our sleds are like snowplows. Animals use the trails we make to move around and find food."

Springtime in Wyoming gradually brings longer and warmer days. Snow half melts, half evaporates all across the state. It is calv-

The breathtaking views and challenging runs of the Tetons attract skiers to Jackson Hole every winter.

ing season, and ranch families work long hours to make sure the newborns are safe. As the grass thickens and warm spring breezes blow, wild animals fatten themselves after the hard winter months.

Summer is short in Wyoming, so people make the most of it. Farmers plant their crops as early as possible and pray for rain. School ends, but many kids settle down to hard work rather than relaxation and television, for Wyoming families tend to work together to get by. Summer is also the busiest time for visiting and celebrating. It is a time of county fairs and the Wyoming State Fair in Douglas.

Wyoming's biggest celebration is Frontier Days, held every July in Cheyenne. Thousands of people attend pancake breakfasts and chili feasts, enjoy the carnival rides, and watch air shows. There is an Indian village run by the Shoshone tribe, with displays of traditional dancing and storytelling, and booths offering Indian crafts and food. But the festival's high point is its rodeo, the oldest in the United States. A rodeo's main events are bronco and steer

This farmer enjoys good working weather near Alta.

Wyoming's Indian tribes preserve their cultural traditions through such events as this powwow at Crowheart.

riding, in which contestants try to stay atop the wild, bucking animals as long as possible. There are also contests to see how quickly competitors can rope and tie calves and steers, and races to see how fast a horse and rider can run figure eights around closely spaced barrels. All these events test traditional cowboy skills (cowgirl skills, too—many competitors are women).

Summer never seems to last long enough in Wyoming. Children return reluctantly to school; farmers spend long days harvesting their crops. Fall is hunting season, though, and Wyoming is full of wildlife. Thousands of people come from other states to hunt antelope, deer, and moose. Strangely, hunting is not particularly popular among Wyomingites. Only about one in ten are hunters, much lower than in many other places. But fishing is very popular. A survey has shown that Riverton and Casper are the third and fourth most enthusiastic fishing towns in the country—four in ten residents of each town consider themselves "frequent anglers."

"Rodeo is the wild child of ranch work," writes rancher Gretel Ehrlich. "Horsemanship—not gunslinging—was the pride of western men."

COWBOY BISCUITS AND ICE CREAM

Hard work builds powerful appetites, so Wyomingites enjoy hearty meals. Here's a Wyoming dessert that is best eaten in a ranch kitchen during a howling blizzard, but you can enjoy it anywhere. Ask an adult to help you with this recipe.

2 cups flour
4 teaspoons baking powder
1 teaspoon salt
2 tablespoons butter
¾ cup milk
1 can sliced peaches in syrup
1 carton vanilla ice cream

Preheat the oven to 450°F. Mix the dry ingredients in a bowl and sift them. Work the butter into the mixture with your fingertips. Add the milk gradually, stirring with a knife to make a soft dough. (If it seems too stiff, add a little more milk.)

On a floured board, flatten the dough to half an inch thick. Use a drinking glass to cut out biscuits (dip it in flour between cuts so it doesn't stick). Place the biscuits on a buttered cookie sheet and bake until golden brown (12–15 minutes).

As soon as the biscuits are done, it's time for dessert. Open a can of sliced peaches in syrup. Place a hot biscuit in a bowl. Surround it with two or three peach slices. Top this with a scoop or two of vanilla ice cream, and drizzle it with a spoonful of the syrup from the peaches. Enjoy it while it's still hot—and cold!

Wyoming is an anglers' delight: clean water and plenty of fish.

THE ACTIVE LIFE

As winter begins again, Wyomingites—whose whole way of life revolves around the outdoors—tend to retreat indoors once again. Even in the winter, though, Wyomingites are active, sometimes in ways that don't fit their frontier image. Wyoming ranks second among the states in the percentage of people who run or jog, and third in the proportion of bicyclists. Wyomingites also visit health clubs and gymnasiums far more frequently than the average American. Along with the tough, active work that most residents do, this makes Wyoming one of the most physically fit states in the nation.

High school sports are also important, especially in Wyoming's smaller communities. In Gillette, the girl's volleyball, cross-country, and swimming teams are often nationally ranked. The girl's basketball team is so good that it travels around the country playing in national tournaments. The key to their success, says coach Russ Hall, is "the community support and the expectations the athletes have for themselves." Ronn Jeffrey, who directs kid's athletic leagues in Cheyenne, agrees: "If you go to a game in Gillette, and you're from out of town, there's a chance you won't get a seat because everyone there goes to the games."

NEW WYOMINGITES

In recent years, more and more people from other parts of the United States have moved to Wyoming. They are attracted by the state's beauty, low crime rate, lack of income tax, and low cost of living. Ed and Jeanne Armintrout moved from California to Laramie several years ago. In California, it took Armintrout ninety minutes to commute from home to work. In Laramie, he says, "there's no traffic, people are great." Jeanne Armintrout recalls that when she got off the plane to visit Laramie for the first time, "I cried because it was so beautiful." The Armintrouts make less money in Wyoming than they did in California, but they don't care. Their children are safer, they think, and the whole family loves their new state. "In some ways we care more about Wyoming than natives do," Jeanne Armintrout says, "because we've seen what happens when things go bad."

Whether newcomers or old-timers, most Wyomingites enjoy

Clean air and empty roads have lured many families to Wyoming.

living in a unique place. The severe weather, isolation, and hard work it takes to live there don't seem like hardships. They are just part of life in the natural wonderland they love.

5 MAKING A MARK

Wyomingites treasure their past. The state's early exploration, settlement, and development overflow with larger-than-life characters—from the Indian guide Sacagawea to that great symbol of western life, Buffalo Bill. Nearly every small Wyoming town seems to have a museum or a historic site that celebrates these early heroes. But some recent Wyomingites have made the state proud as well.

NATIVE AMERICANS

One of the first Wyomingites to have contact with the larger world was Sacagawea, a Shoshone woman whose help was crucial to the Lewis and Clark expedition during their journey across the West.

Sacagawea was born in Wyoming around 1784. When she was a child, she was captured by Minnetarre Indians and taken away from her people's lands. She married a French explorer and lived in the Dakotas until 1805, when Lewis and Clark arrived and asked her to guide their expedition.

Sacagawea ably brought the expedition through country she had not seen since childhood and helped negotiate safe passage for them with the Shoshones. On the way she gave birth to a son and adopted the child of her dead sister. They were the only children on the expedition, and she was the only woman. She led Lewis and

Sacagawea guided Lewis and Clark to the Pacific coast, helping the United States to take possession of the West.

Clark all the way to the Pacific Ocean and then back through the Yellowstone area as they returned east. In Minnetarre country, she left the expedition, leaving Lewis and Clark to describe her exploits back in Washington, D.C.

Little of Sacagawea's life after this is known. She lived through the coming of more explorers, settlers, and soldiers, and reappeared as an elderly woman on the Wind River Indian Reservation. When she died there in 1884, she had witnessed a century of enormous change.

Many Indian leaders played important roles during the decades of contact and conflict with the newcomers from the East. One was a great Shoshone chief, Washakie, whose valor is the subject of many stories. Legend has it that after years of fighting between the Shoshones and Crows over who could hunt on the lands sur-

Washakie, the great Shoshone chief. His diplomacy helped his people avoid the worst effects of the clash between settlers and Indians.

rounding Crowheart Butte, Washakie challenged the Crow chief to a fight to settle the matter once and for all. Washakie won the battle and then cut out his opponent's heart and ate it, giving Crowheart Butte its name. Years later a cowboy asked Washakie if the story was true. "When you're young and full of life," he answered, "you do strange things."

But Washakie is mainly remembered not as a warrior and a heart-eater, but as a diplomat—a peacemaker between the Shoshones and the settlers. Washakie knew that the settlers would not disappear. Instead of mourning the loss of the Shoshones' nomadic way of life, Washakie worked to secure land and return his people to the agricultural lifestyle they had known centuries earlier.

THE GOVERNMENT DOES NOT KEEP ITS WORD

At age eighty, Chief Washakie told Wyoming territorial governor John Hoyt of his anguish over the American government's treatment of the Shoshones:

> The white man, who possesses this whole vast country from sea to sea, who roams over it at pleasure, and lives where he likes, cannot know the cramp we feel in this little spot, with the undying remembrance of the fact . . . that every foot of what you proudly call America, not very long ago belonged to the red man.
>
> The white man's government promised that if we, the Shoshones, would be content with the little patch allowed us, it would keep us well supplied with everything necessary for comfortable living, and see that no white man should cross our borders for our game, or anything else that is ours. *But it has not kept its word!* The white man kills our game, captures our furs, and sometimes feeds his herds upon our meadows. . . . Knowing all this, do you wonder, sir, that we have fits of depression and think to be avenged!

Washakie worked hard to keep the Shoshones out of the bloody conflicts of the 1850s and 1860s. He negotiated the treaty that created the Wind River Indian Reservation and built trust between his tribe and the U.S. government. When war again broke out between the U.S. Army and the Lakota Indians in the mid-1870s, Washakie led over two hundred Shoshone warriors into battle against the Dakotas. He was in his seventies, yet he continued to assist the army as a scout for twenty more years. Washakie died in

1900. He had compromised more than other Indian leaders, but the Shoshones probably suffered less as a result. Washakie died a disappointed man, however, because his people would never again enjoy the freedom they had had before the coming of the settlers.

THE FACE OF THE WILD WEST

William F. Cody, or "Buffalo Bill," earned his nickname from a dark part of his career—his role in the slaughter of the bison herds. But he was also a scout and an entertainer, and his Wild West show made him the West's best-known figure by the end of the nineteenth century.

Buffalo Bill's family moved to Wyoming when he was a small boy. His father died when he was eleven, and Bill got a job as a messenger to help support his family. Later, he became a rider for the Pony Express, a mail delivery service, once galloping 320 miles in less than a day—the longest Pony Express ride ever. During the Civil War, he was a Union army scout. Afterward, he became a hunter, supplying meat to the crews building the transcontinental railroad. This is when he became famous as "Buffalo Bill," the greatest bison hunter in the West.

His exploits during the Indian wars of the 1860s caught the attention of eastern newspapers, and Buffalo Bill became a national celebrity. He put together his Wild West show, which toured the United States and Europe, dazzling audiences with its romantic displays of life on the frontier. Annie Oakley, a crack pistol shooter, and even the defeated Lakota chief Sitting Bull joined the show. Buffalo Bill and Sitting Bull, enemies in war, became friends in peace.

For most Americans, Buffalo Bill Cody represented the Wild West— from bison hunting and Indian fighting to his celebrated shows.

Buffalo Bill's show made him rich. He bought a ranch east of Yellowstone Park and helped establish the nearby town of Cody— named, of course, after him. But the hunter, scout, and showman was no businessman. The Wild West show went bankrupt, and Buffalo Bill died almost broke. He had wanted to be buried on his ranch, but his widow accepted ten thousand dollars from a business partner to allow Bill to be buried near Denver, Colorado. The partner had truckloads of concrete poured over Bill's grave to keep the famous body in Colorado forever.

OUTLAWS

Two of Wyoming's most famous characters were its most notorious outlaws, Butch Cassidy and the Sundance Kid. Cassidy started his

The Hole-in-the-Wall Gang pose for a respectable photograph. Butch Cassidy is seated at right; the Sundance Kid is seated at left.

life of crime as a cattle rustler, but soon found bank and train robbery more profitable. He joined Harry Longabaugh (the Sundance Kid) and other desperadoes to form the Hole-in-the-Wall Gang, named after a favorite hideout near Kaycee.

Cassidy was caught stealing horses near Lander in 1894 and spent two years in prison. When he was released, the gang went back to its old ways. By 1901, the law was closing in on him again, and he and the Sundance Kid fled to South America, where they went on robbing banks and trains. Some say the pair perished in a shoot-out in Bolivia, but others claim they returned to live out their lives in Wyoming. Francis Smith, a Wyoming doctor, remembered how an old man appeared in his doorway in the 1920s. "You don't know who I am, do you?" asked the man. "You look familiar," replied the doctor, "but I can't quite say." The man displayed a surgical scar on his belly, which the doctor recognized as his own work. His face had been altered by plastic surgery, but, Smith insisted, the man was Butch Cassidy.

A WYOMINGITE IN WASHINGTON

Some of the most noteworthy Wyomingites in recent years have been its politicians in Washington. Alan Simpson, a senator from 1978 to 1996, is the quintessential Wyoming politician.

Al was raised in Cody and played football at the University of Wyoming before becoming a lawyer and then a leading member of the Wyoming state legislature. He also helped his father become governor of Wyoming. In 1978, Al ran for U.S. senator and won. Almost immediately, he became a political celebrity in Washington, with his cowboy humor and colorful, though sometimes abrasive, personality. "I wear a size fifteen shoe," he once said, "and I'm about to put my foot in my mouth." He was a serious senator, best known as an advocate for reforming immigration laws and as a scathing critic of how the media presents political news. Simpson retired from the Senate in 1996. His plans? "I want to make some money," he joked. "I'm going to get an agent."

ENTERTAINERS

Some celebrated Wyomingites, like many average citizens, have come to the state from somewhere else. One good example is actor Harrison Ford, who grew up in Illinois and lived for years in California before moving to Wyoming.

Ford began trying to break into movies soon after college, but it was a long struggle. He landed small parts in several second-rate movies and television shows, but he had better luck as the "carpenter to the stars," doing construction jobs for Hollywood celebrities.

Harrison Ford is just one of the many Hollywood stars who have moved to Wyoming to escape the hustle and bustle of Los Angeles.

He never stopped trying to be an actor, though. His lucky break came when he was cast as Han Solo, the interstellar smuggler who is the reluctant hero of *Star Wars*. Suddenly, Ford was a Hollywood superstar. Two more Star Wars films followed, and then *Raiders of the Lost Ark*, in which he played Indiana Jones, an anthropology professor turned daring adventurer. By the time he had appeared in two more Indiana Jones movies, he was the best-known action movie star of his generation. "You cannot get where I got without luck," says Ford. "Bags of it." But luck was not enough: "I persisted. And other people gave up."

Harrison Ford doesn't much like Hollywood. In the 1980s, he bought land near Jackson and built a ranch. He helped build the house himself, using his hard-won experience as a carpenter. Ford loves Wyoming and takes full advantage of his adopted state. He spends his time between films hiking, fishing, and riding horses.

Music is probably the most important art in Wyoming. Cowboy ballads and country music have always been popular, since they celebrate the outdoor, high country life of the American West. Not many country musicians have lived that life as fully as Wyoming's Chris LeDoux, who was a rodeo champion before he became a country music star.

LeDoux caught the cowboy bug when he was very young and set his heart on making it big in the rodeo. His hopes and hard work were rewarded when, at age sixteen, he won the Little Britches world championship for bareback bronco riding. After college, LeDoux spent years riding the rodeo circuit. In 1976, he achieved his greatest goal: winning the world championship for bareback bronco riding.

Chris LeDoux says his career "started out as just rodeo stuff." Now he is a genuine country music star.

While he was competing in rodeos, LeDoux was also writing songs. He began selling cassettes of his music at rodeos. Now that the rodeo champ is retired, the country star and his band, Western Underground, tour all over the country. Their music mixes country and rock, and their shows feature fireworks and other pyrotechnics. Garth Brooks, a country superstar who has recorded with LeDoux, says, "He's like a rocker with a cowboy hat on."

Having recorded about thirty albums, LeDoux is Wyoming's biggest music star. Despite his fame, he still lives on a ranch near Kaycee and celebrates his state's unique way of life in his songs:

> I got peace of mind and elbowroom
> I love to smell the sage in bloom
> Or catch a rainbow on my fishin' line
> We've got country fairs and rodeos
> There ain't a better place for my kids to grow
> Just turn 'em loose in the western summertime.

6 A FANTASTIC VOYAGE

Picture a box with a big letter S drawn inside it. The box is Wyoming, and the S is a tour of the state. The box isn't really a box; it's many different places and people. It is mountains and plains, towns and ranches, old settlements and new, changing landscapes. Let's make a voyage to visit them.

BLACK HILLS AND BIGHORNS

Beginning at the top of the S, in the upper right-hand corner of the state, we start in the Black Hills, a group of small mountains covered by dark pine forests. Most of the Black Hills are in South Dakota, but some extend into Wyoming. Dakotas and other Indians have long regarded the Black Hills as holy, including Devils Tower—a huge knuckle of fluted volcanic rock rising above the grasslands. Devils Tower is well known to those who have seen the movie *Close Encounters of the Third Kind* as the spot where an alien spaceship lands. Since that movie was made, more and more people have visited the tower, including many rock climbers who enjoy the challenge of scrambling up the channels in its surface.

As we travel west through the northern grasslands, the dramatic Bighorn Mountains rise on the horizon. At their foot is Sheridan, a busy town that grew up around the cattle industry and still celebrates the ranching lifestyle with rodeos and cattle drives every

Eerie Devils Tower rises over the plains of northeastern Wyoming.

summer. On its outskirts is the Eaton Ranch, one of the grandest of the old dude ranches, where droves of eastern tourists played cowboy in the early twentieth century. It's still open to guests. The Bighorns rise steeply from Sheridan—beautiful mountains of yellow and brown surrounding valleys dotted with such flowers as Indian paintbrush and wild rose.

Beyond the mountains, the land flattens into Bighorn Basin, a dry expanse of sagebrush and sky. Near the town of Lovell is Wyoming's most important Indian artifact: the Medicine Wheel,

THE STORY OF DEVILS TOWER

Here is a Dakota legend of how Devils Tower came to be:

After a long day of travel, an Indian tribe stopped on a river-bank. Seven small girls went off to play while their parents made camp. The girls wandered through the tall grasses, chasing each other farther and farther from camp.

Suddenly, they stumbled upon a slumbering bear. The bear awoke and began chasing them. The girls fled toward camp, but they could see that the bear was going to catch them. As they sprinted through the tall grass, they came upon a big rock. They scrambled onto it and began to pray: "Oh, Rock, take pity on us!"

The rock heard the girls' pleas. It rose out of the ground, lifting them out of the bear's reach. The bear lunged again and again at the rock as it grew, breaking his claws as he tried to scramble toward the girls. The rock became a lofty tower, marked everywhere by the bear's scratches. The girls were pushed into the sky, where they became seven little stars—the ones that make up the constellation we now call the Pleiades. The bear stalked off through the grass and disappeared, but the tower remains.

a large circle of rocks on a high table of land with twenty-eight "spokes" radiating from its center. It is an ancient site, at least a thousand years old. Its purpose is a mystery, for the culture that built it disappeared long ago. Today's Indians have adopted it as a holy site and conduct religious ceremonies there.

Across the Bighorn Basin is the town of Cody, which is a monument to its founder, Buffalo Bill. Cody's western flavor and museums make it one of the most popular tourist destinations in Wyoming. The Buffalo Bill Museum is full of objects from Bill's life, including firearms, cowboy gear, and souvenirs from the Wild West show. The Plains Indian Museum features displays on many Indian tribes, including art and artifacts of everyday life, like tepees and weapons used for hunting bison. On the outskirts of Cody is Old Trail Town, a street lined with old houses and buildings rescued from around the state and moved here for display—including Butch Cassidy's cabin from the Hole-in-the-Wall.

Riders tear through the Shoshone National Forest in northeastern Wyoming.

The Medicine Wheel is something of a mystery.
Who built it and for "exactly what purpose" have
been "lost in time," says writer Nathaniel Burt.

The buildings of old Wyoming have been preserved
at Old Trail Town, on the outskirts of Cody.

Though Cheyenne disputes it, Cody claims to be the Rodeo Capital of the World. The Cody Nite Rodeo takes place every evening during the summer, and kids' riding and roping events are a big part of the action. Cody also calls itself the Gateway to Yellowstone, and no one disputes that. The highway west of town wriggles through narrow Shoshone Canyon, cutting close to the roaring Shoshone River and disappearing into long, dark tunnels blasted through the cliffs that loom alongside it. Fifty miles from Cody, the road reaches the east gate of Wyoming's greatest treasure.

YELLOWSTONE AND THE WESTERN MOUNTAINS

Created in 1872, Yellowstone is the nation's oldest national park, and its most popular. More than three million people visit the park every summer. The park contains some ten thousand "thermal features," from geysers that spew out water and steam to bubbling mudpots and boiling mineral springs. Old Faithful, which erupts almost every hour, is the most famous. Most Yellowstone geysers erupt less frequently, but some of them are much more powerful. Giant Geyser shoots a plume of hot water skyward every ten days or so. Its eruptions last up to an hour and can eject a million gallons of water. "It's really something you don't want to miss," says Ann Deutsch, a Yellowstone naturalist.

Wyoming's most famous landmark is Old Faithful, the geyser that keeps its appointments with the tourists.

Another Yellowstone highlight is seeing the herds of bison and other wildlife, including grizzly bears and wolves. Adventurous types hike far into Yellowstone's forests and mountains, discovering sights that car-bound travelers can only imagine. In the winter, they ski or snowshoe to their destinations—most park roads close with the coming of snow. Some Yellowstone visitors camp, and others stay in hotels like the Old Faithful Inn, the world's largest log building. During the summer many young people work at Yellowstone's hotels and campgrounds, or at jobs maintaining trails or serving as guides. "It's the best possible summer job in the country," says Joseph Luders, a student from Washington State.

Passing south out of Yellowstone, we arrive at the Teton Range. Grand Teton National Park is less developed than Yellowstone. It is a haven for hiking, horseback riding, and wildlife watching, as well as white-water rafting and fishing. The Tetons also attract thousands of mountain climbers every year. The snowcapped peaks stand alongside Jackson Hole, a spectacular valley containing Jackson and Jenny Lakes. The town of Jackson has become a popular place for wealthy newcomers.

As we head back east from Jackson on our S-shaped tour, we hit a giant roadblock, the Wind River Range. No road crosses it, so we must navigate around it. Surrounding the range is the Wind River Indian Reservation, shared by Shoshone and Arapaho Indians. This is a remote area, and few non-Indians visit it. Backpackers and mountain climbers see much more of this magnificent range and its glaciers, lakes, and meadows than car travelers do.

The reservation is dotted with very small settlements and a few towns. In one of them, Ethete, is St. Michael's Mission, a circle of

Mountain climbers love Grand Teton National Park, but so do hikers without ropes and fancy climbing equipment.

buildings that includes the striking Church of Our Father's House. The church is adorned with Indian crafts and designs. Its altar is a large drum, and the window behind it looks out on the rising sun and the mountains. Another town, Fort Washakie, features the graves of both Chief Washakie and Sacagawea.

The Wind River flows north out of the reservation and plunges through Wind River Canyon, another spectacular sight. The narrow cliffs are a thousand feet high on both sides of the churning river and cast the whole canyon into deep shadows when the sun is not directly overhead.

Nearby is the town of Thermopolis and its main attraction, Hot Springs State Park. The park contains the world's largest mineral hot springs, which discharge four million gallons of hot water every day from a multicolored pool banked by dripping mineral deposits. The water feeds a large outdoor swimming pool, which stays warm enough to attract bathers even during winter blizzards. It's a weird sight: bathing suits, cowboy hats, whirling snowflakes falling, and thick clouds of steam rising to meet them.

BACKWARD ALONG THE OREGON TRAIL

Heading east takes us out of the mountains and back onto the plains along a stretch of the Oregon Trail. There we can visit Independence Rock and many other landmarks that guided the pioneers. At Martin's Cove, disaster struck a company of Mormons pushing handcarts toward Utah in late 1856. Snow, cold, disease, and hunger brought them to a halt there. A rescue team sent from Salt Lake City saved many lives, but at least a hundred died and were buried at Martin's Cove. "Please stay on the paths," signs read. "Many graves are unidentified."

Casper, the first of the three "big" cities on our tour, thrived during the oil boom of the 1970s and early 1980s, and it looks newly built compared to Wyoming's many Old West towns. From

PLACES TO SEE

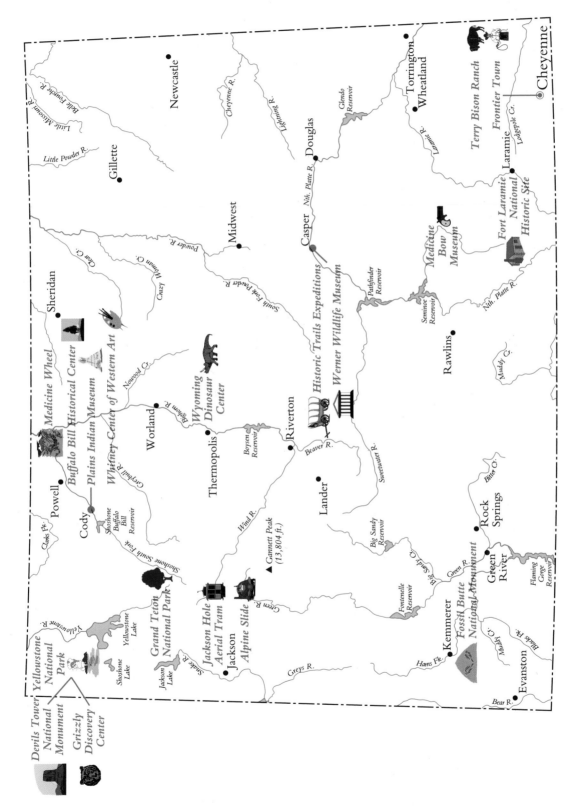

Cheyenne

Newcastle

Torrington
Wheatland

Terry Bison Ranch
Frontier Town

Gillette

Douglas

Fort Laramie
National
Historic Site

Laramie

Midwest

Casper

Medicine
Bow
Museum

Sheridan

Historic Trails Expeditions
Werner Wildlife Museum

Rawlins

Medicine Wheel

Buffalo Bill Historical Center

Plains Indian Museum

Whitney Center of Western Art

Wyoming
Dinosaur
Center

Worland

Riverton

Powell

Cody

Thermopolis

Lander

Rock
Springs

▲ Gannett Peak
(13,804 ft.)

Green
River

Jackson Hole
Aerial Tram

Jackson
Alpine Slide

Kemmerer

Fossil Butte
National Monument

Evanston

Devils Tower
National
Monument

Grizzly
Discovery
Center

Yellowstone National
Park

Grand Teton
National Park

THE MORMON TRAIL RE-ENACTMENT

In 1997, Mormons marked the 150th anniversary of their migration to Salt Lake City with a re-enactment of the historic journey. Beginning in Omaha, Nebraska, a parade of wagons and handcarts followed the old trails across Nebraska and Wyoming to Utah. The three-month journey crossed a thousand miles of plains, mountains, and desert.

Over 150 Mormons, from small children to eighty-one-year-old Steve Ellis, participated in the re-enactment. Oxen, horses, and mules pulled the wagons, but the dozen handcarts that joined them were pulled by people, just as they were originally. The wagon train spent six weeks crossing Wyoming, visiting historic sites along the way. At Fort Bridger, a newcomer joined the group when a baby, Henry Freestone Bentley, was born. "It's not too different from delivering at home," his mother said, "except I couldn't shower."

About six thousand Mormons died making this journey between 1847 and 1869. But many thousands more survived to build Salt Lake City and the state of Utah. Many who took part in the re-enactment were inspired by the hardships of their ancestors. "We've studied the pioneers," said one participant, "and the lessons they learned are ones I want my children to learn."

Casper we zoom south to the oldest settled corner of Wyoming. The speed limit on Wyoming's highways is seventy-five miles per hour, but it still takes more than two hours to reach Cheyenne. It's even longer if we stop along the way—perhaps in Douglas, to see the town's giant statue of a jackelope (a mythical animal that has the body of a rabbit and the antlers of an antelope).

Another tempting stop is Fort Laramie National Historic Site, which was built as a trading post in 1834 and became a military fort in 1849 to protect travelers on the Oregon Trail. The fort is the best-preserved relic of early settlement and military life in Wyoming. It has "the feeling of what it really must have been like then," says writer Nathaniel Burt. Many of the original buildings have been restored, including a bunkhouse called Old Bedlam, which housed rowdy soldiers. Built in 1849, it is the oldest building in the state.

ALONG THE UNION PACIFIC LINE

At Cheyenne we turn the final corner of our tour. Cheyenne was the first major city built as the Union Pacific Railroad began advancing across Wyoming in 1867. In the center of Cheyenne is Wyoming's capitol, which was finished just in time for statehood in 1890. Built of gray and tan stone, it looks solid and practical, like Wyoming—not like the gleaming white capitols in many other states.

Traveling west along the Union Pacific tracks takes us through the last mountain pass of our voyage, one of the windiest places in the United States. Sometimes Interstate 80, the freeway here, is closed for no other reason than the peril of whipping gusts. The wind has eroded the Vedauwoo rock formations between Cheyenne and Laramie into an eerie panorama of rounded, piled stones. They look like loaves of bread and rolls stacked in a bakery window.

Laramie, forty-nine miles west of Cheyenne, is the home of the University of Wyoming and its geological museum. Among its exhibits is the gigantic skeleton of a brontosaurus, a native of

The Vedauwoo rocks are a monument to the power of wind, which carved these weird formations over thousands of years.

Wyoming's prehistoric swamps, and the largest dinosaur ever discovered. Outside the museum stands a full-scale statue of tyrannosaurus rex, the fiercest dinosaur ever to roam Wyoming—or anywhere else.

West of Laramie is Rawlins, the site of the Wyoming State Prison, a forbidding building that closed in 1982 and is now a museum. Visitors can sit inside the old gas chamber, where five prisoners were executed over the years. (If you want, they'll strap you into the chair and close the door!) At night, visitors feel their way through the prison on tours conducted in total darkness.

Rawlins is perched at the edge of the Red Desert and the Great Divide Basin. Very few people live there, but you are likely to see an abundance of wildlife, including some of the largest herds of pronghorn antelope and wild horses. On its western edge, the steady wind has created the Killpecker Sand Dunes.

The Killpecker Sand Dunes are the largest active sand dunes—where the wind blows the dunes along—outside of Africa's Sahara Desert.

This corner of Wyoming is raw, dry, and flat—at least flat compared to other places in the state. Around the towns of Green River and Rock Springs are some of Wyoming's biggest mines, and even from the highway you can see the massive scale of these operations.

Just south of these towns is a fine place to relax and rest from our voyage around the state: Flaming Gorge. Carved by the Green

Once a wild canyon on the Green River, Flaming Gorge is now a huge man-made reservoir. The severe colorful landscape that surrounds it is still one of Wyoming's most stunning vistas.

River over millions of years, the gorge was named for its brilliantly colored rock and the sculpted land surrounding it. Once the Green River roared through the gorge, but now it is a huge reservoir, thanks to a controversial dam in Utah. The dam transformed the steep-walled river canyon into a ninety-mile-long lake. Though many Wyomingites regret the loss of that unique landscape, others flock to the new Flaming Gorge with speedboats and fishing tackle, for it is an angler's hot spot filled with trout and other fish. Even though much of its former glory is underwater, it is still one of the most beautiful places in Wyoming—perhaps in the world.

There, we've drawn our S—a long voyage that could be taken by car, train, bicycle, horse, snowshoe, or airplane. We have only imagined the journey. Start planning now for the real thing!

THE FLAG: *Adopted in 1917, the state flag depicts a buffalo with the state seal "branded" on its side. The blue background has two borders: white symbolizing purity and red standing for the Indians and the blood of pioneers.*

THE SEAL: *The state seal, adopted in 1893, shows a woman and the motto "Equal Rights." They symbolize Wyoming's early commitment to civil rights for women. A cowboy and a miner stand next to her, representing the state's two important industries, livestock and mining.*

STATE SURVEY

STATE SURVEY

Statehood: July 10, 1890

Origin of Name: From the Algonquin Indian phrase *Maugh-wau-wa-ma*, meaning "large plains" or from the Delaware Indian phrase for "mountains and valleys alternating."

Nickname: Equality State

Capital: Cheyenne

Motto: Equal Rights

Bird: Meadowlark

Flower: Indian paintbrush

Tree: Cottonwood

Gem: Jade

Fish: Cutthroat trout

Mammal: Bison

Meadowlark

Indian paintbrush

WYOMING MARCH SONG

In the summer of 1903, Judge Charles E. Winter of Casper wrote a poem entitled "Wyoming." It wasn't until the 1920s that George E. Knapp, the director of the music department of the University of Wyoming at Laramie, set the poem to music. Another 30 years passed before the "Wyoming March Song" was adopted as the official state song in 1955.

Words by Charles E. Winter **Music by George E. Knapp**

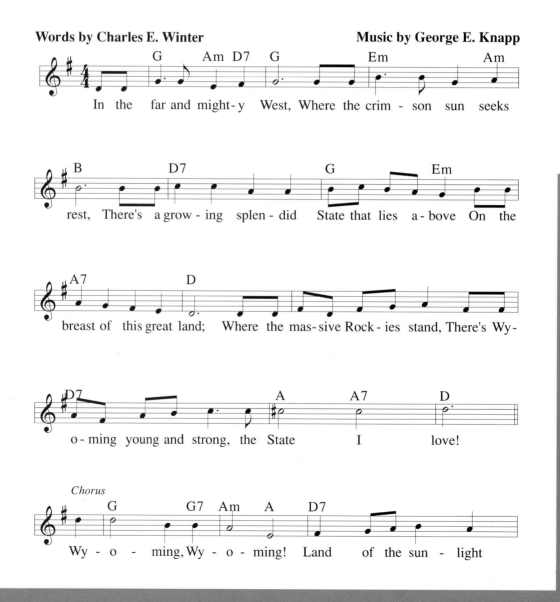

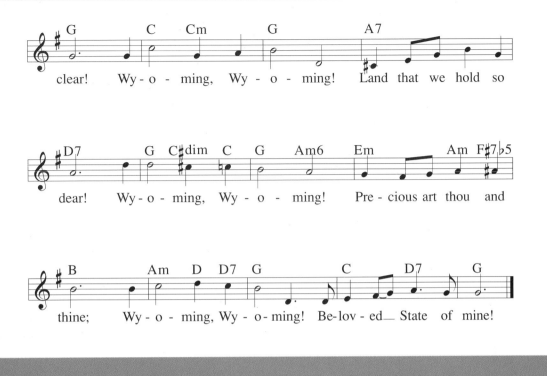

Reptile: Horned toad

Fossil: Knightia

Dinosaur: Triceratops

GEOGRAPHY

Highest point: 13,804 feet above sea level at Gannett Peak

Lowest point: 3,100 feet at Belle Fourche River in Crook County

Area: 97,818 square miles

Greatest Distance, North to South: 275 miles

Greatest Distance, East to West: 362 miles

Bordering States: Montana to the north and west, South Dakota and Nebraska to the east, Colorado to the south, Utah to the south and west, Idaho to the west

Hottest Recorded Temperature: 114°F at Basin on July 12, 1900

Coldest Recorded Temperature: -66°F at Moran on February 9, 1933

Average Annual Precipitation: 13 inches

Major Rivers: Bighorn, Green, North Platte, Powder, Snake, Yellowstone

Major Lakes: Bighorn, Flaming Gorge, Pathfinder, Saratoga, Yellowstone

Trees: aspen, cottonwood, Douglas fir, Engelmann spruce, lodgepole pine, ponderosa pine, subalpine fir

Wild Plants: arnica, bluegrass, buttercup, cactus, evening star, five-finger, flax, forget-me-not, goldenrod, redtop, sagebrush, saxifrage, sour dock, tufted fescue, wheat grass, windflower

Animals: beaver, black bear, coyote, elk, fox, grizzly bear, lynx, marten, moose, mountain lion, mule deer, pronghorn, raccoon, otter, white-tailed deer

Birds: bald eagle, duck, golden eagle, goose, grouse, pheasant, sage hen, wild turkey

Fish: bass, bluegill, channel catfish, crappie, saugerling, trout, walleye

Endangered Animals: American peregrine falcon, bald eagle, black-footed ferret, Colorado squawfish, gray

Black-footed ferret

wolf, grizzly bear, Kendall Warm Springs dace, razorbook sucker, whooping crane, Wyoming toad

Endangered Plant: Ute ladies' tresses

TIMELINE

Wyoming History

1500s Shoshones, Arapahos, Lakotas, Crows, Cheyennes, Bannocks, and Northern Utes live in the region

1807 John Colter explores Yellowstone area

1812 Robert Stuart discovers South Pass as route through Rocky Mountains

1832 First wagons travel Oregon Trail through South Pass, opening the West to settlers

1834 William Sublette and Robert Campbell establish Fort William (later renamed Fort Laramie), the first permanent trading post in Wyoming

1843 Fort Bridger, Wyoming's second permanent settlement, is established

1860s Tension along Powder River erupts into fighting between settlers and Indians

1861 Transcontinental telegraph completed, providing speedy communication between East and West Coasts

1863 Bozeman Trail to Montana mines opened

1866 Chief Red Cloud and Lakotas surprise a U.S. cavalry group, killing all 81 soldiers

1867 Union Pacific Railroad enters Wyoming; Cheyenne founded

1868 U.S. Congress creates Wyoming Territory; treaty between U.S. and Indians signed at Fort Laramie, creating reservation for Indians and allowing U.S. to build roads and railroads

1869 Wyoming legislature gives women the right to vote and hold office

1870 Esther Morris becomes first female justice of the peace in the United States

1872 Yellowstone becomes the world's first national park

1876 War breaks out between U.S. and Indians as thousands of settlers invade Indian lands in search of gold; U.S. troops destroy Cheyenne camp along Powder River, leaving Indians to freeze or starve

1883 First oil well drilled in Wyoming

1890 Wyoming becomes 44th state

1892 Cattle rustling dispute between large cattle ranchers and smaller ranchers erupts into the Johnson County War

1906 Devils Tower becomes first national monument

1918 Uranium discovered near Lusk

1924 Nellie Tayloe Ross becomes first woman governor in United States

1929 Grand Teton National Park opens

1951–1952 Major uranium deposits discovered in many parts of state

1958 Nation's first operational intercontinental ballistic missile base opens near Cheyenne

1978 Largest radio telescope in world built on Jelm Mountain

1988 Fire damages more than 1 million acres in Yellowstone National Park

1989 Wyomingite Richard Cheney becomes U.S. secretary of defense

ECONOMY

Agricultural Products: beef cattle, corn, dairy products, sheep, sugar beets, wheat

Manufactured Products: chemicals, glass and clay products, lumber and wood products, petroleum products

Natural Resources: bentonite, coal, iron ore, natural gas, petroleum, stone, trona

Business and Trade: communications, tourism, transportation, utilities

Sheep

CALENDAR OF CELEBRATIONS

Wyoming State Winter Fair Lander breaks up Wyoming's long, brutal winter with a celebration in late January. Highlights include horse, cat, dog, and even llama shows. The musical entertainment, food, and fun take the chill off.

International Rocky Mountain Stage Stop Sled Dog Race In February, a 400-mile dogsled race winds through nine Wyoming counties. Each night, the teams stop in a different town, which greets the hearty human and canine racers with food and enthusiasm.

Days of '49 During the second weekend of June, Greybull hosts its "Boots, Hooves, and Wheels Rodeo," featuring a traditional rodeo, parades, demolition derby, and other family events. Why is it called Days of '49? The Greybull Jaycees first held this big weekend in 1949.

Bozeman Trail Days The cavalry rides again for three days every June when Story celebrates 100 years of Wyoming history. Retrace the dangerous route of gold-seeking settlers who took a shortcut through Indian lands. Watch colorful cavalry exhibitions and Native American dancing.

Mustang Days Modern-day cowboys and cowgirls rope steers and ride bucking broncos and angry bulls at this classic rodeo in Lovell during the last week of June. The event also includes a chuckwagon breakfast, parades, street dancing, a family fun festival, a demolition derby, a barbecue, and, to top it all off, fireworks.

Ten Sleep Rodeo Days For the past 50 years, Fourth of July in Ten Sleep has been rodeo time. And when the sun sets, tourists, rodeo riders, and townspeople enjoy an old-fashioned street dance.

Sheepherder's Rodeo Each July, Kaycee proves you *can* have a rodeo without cattle. This sheep rodeo features sheep-roping, sheep-riding, and sheep-hooking. You can also watch sheepdogs at work—responding only to signals from their owners, they separate and pen a designated number of sheep.

Pioneer Days During the third week of July, the people of Cowley celebrate their pioneer heritage with parades, dancing, a rodeo, and other contests. This event has also become a traditional time for family and school reunions in Cowley.

Cheyenne Frontier Days If you can't get enough of rodeo excitement, come to Cheyenne's Frontier Days in July for a week of roping, bucking, and riding. Each day after the rodeo ends, the famous Frontier Days Wild Horse Race pits teams of amateur cowboys against young, unbroken broncos. Parades during the week feature the world's largest collection of horse-drawn vehicles, along with antique carriages, floats, marching bands, clowns, and drill teams. You can also get a free breakfast of flapjacks and ham during the event. In 1996, 39,111 people ate free in one day! The midway offers carnival rides, games, entertainment, and food.

Dayton Days At the end of July, Dayton hosts three days of fun, including a parade, Indian dancing, contests, street entertainment and dances, and food and craft booths. On the last day, the town sponsors a hamburger feed.

Washakie County Fair In August, Worland hosts a humdinger of a county fair, complete with 4-H livestock exhibits, homegrown crops, and cooking contests—and that's just for starters. Big-name country singers such as Reba McIntyre perform at this fair, and you'll also enjoy the classic car show and a great rodeo.

Johnson County Fair and Rodeo The activities of the 4-H clubs take center stage at this county fair in Buffalo each August. A favorite contest features children and sheep dressed in coordinating costumes. Both youth and local ranchers compete in rodeos. The parade includes a fascinating assortment of horses, buggies, pack animals, floats, and people in costume.

Bighorn Mountain Polka Days You'll have a hard time standing still when you hear the lively music of great polka bands. Polka dancers from more than 25 states and Canada come to Sheridan for the three-day Labor Day weekend to celebrate this dance.

Harvest Festival Worland celebrates its farming heritage early in September with a pie-eating contest, beet carving, food booths, crafts, and street dancing. It's a friendly, small town carnival.

Beet carving

STATE STARS

John Bozeman (1835–1867) explored the American West during the 1860s. He was born in Georgia and traveled westward to the Colorado Territory in search of gold. In 1862, he heard about a gold strike in western Montana, and searched for a more direct route there. He traveled what became the Bozeman Trail through Wyoming past the Bighorn Mountains. The U.S. Army soon built a series of forts along this trail.

James Bridger

John Bozeman

James Bridger (1804–1881) was one of the West's most famous mountain men. Born in Virginia, he moved to Illinois when he was eight. As a teen, he took part in a trapping expedition. He and four partners later bought the Rocky Mountain Fur Company. Between 1838 and 1843, he planned and built Fort Bridger on the Green River, which became an important trading post, military post, and Pony Express station. He also served as a guide on several expeditions. Bridger is also believed to have been the first white person to visit the Great Salt Lake.

Richard Cheney (1941–) was U.S. secretary of defense from 1989 to 1993 under President George Bush. He also held an advisory position in Richard Nixon's administration and was chief of staff to President Gerald Ford. Cheney served five terms as a U.S. representative from Wyoming and was a staunch advocate of strengthening national defense.

He was born in Lincoln, Nebraska, and moved to Wyoming as a young child.

Richard Cheney

John Colter (1775–1813), born in Virginia, was a fur trader and guide. In 1807, he explored the area that is now Yellowstone National Park and was the first to return east with tales of the region's steaming geysers. Before that journey, he had taken part in the Lewis and Clark expedition.

June Etta Downey (1875–1932), born in Laramie, was a psychologist and author. She attended and taught at the University of Wyoming. Downey was a pioneer in the study of personality, and she also researched imagination and creativity, color blindness, and handwriting. She wrote many books about her research, as well as works of poetry.

Curt Gowdy (1919–   ), a sportscaster, was born in Green River and graduated from the University of Wyoming. In 1943, he began his career as a sportswriter and local radio broadcaster. From 1951 to 1965, he was the voice of the Boston Red Sox. He went on to cover National Football League games, the Super Bowl, the World Series, and many other sporting events on NBC. He also hosted ABC's *Wide World of Sports* and *American Sportsman*. Gowdy was named to the Sports Broadcasters' Hall of Fame in 1981.

Jacques Laramie (1785?–1821), a trapper, was probably born in Canada. In 1819, he traveled to the unexplored southeastern part of Wyoming. He is believed to be the first white person to see the upper portion of the river that is named for him.

Esther Morris (1814–1902), born in New York, settled in Wyoming Territory in 1869. She is called the mother of women's suffrage in Wyoming because she was active in winning the right to vote for women in Wyoming—the first place in the U.S. where women won that right. In 1870, she became the first female justice of the peace in the United States.

Bill Nye (1850–1896) was a journalist and an important American humorist in the late 19th century. He was born in Maine and moved to Wisconsin as a child. He settled in Laramie in 1876 and began contributing to the *Denver Tribune* and the *Cheyenne Sun*. His humor in the *Laramie Boomerang*, which he helped found in 1881, was widely reprinted. His collections of columns were published in several books, including *Bill Nye and Boomerang* and *Bill Nye's History of the U.S.*

James Cash Penney (1870–1971) founded the J. C. Penney chain of department stores. He was born in Missouri, and in 1897 moved to Colorado where he worked in a dry goods store. In 1902, he was sent to Kemmerer,

James Cash Penney

Wyoming, to open a second store. He invested in the store and soon bought out his partners. Seven years later, he had three stores; by 1924, he had 500. When he died, there were more than 1,600 J. C. Penney stores.

Jackson Pollock (1912–1956), an important American artist, was born in Cody, Wyoming. Pollock moved to New York City in 1929 to study art. He developed his own innovative techniques and style, pouring, dripping, and flinging paint onto his canvases. Pollock's paintings, masterpieces of abstract impressionism, transformed American art.

Nellie Tayloe Ross (1876–1977) became the nation's first woman governor in 1924 when she was elected to finish her deceased husband's term

as governor of Wyoming. In 1933, President Franklin D. Roosevelt named Ross the first female director of the U.S. Mint. During her tenure, the Roosevelt dime and Jefferson nickel were introduced. She was born in Missouri.

Nellie Tayloe Ross

Alan K. Simpson (1931–   ), a Republican senator, was born in Colorado and grew up in Cody. His father, Milward, was governor of Wyoming from 1955 to 1959. Simpson received his undergraduate and law degrees from the University of Wyoming. He served in the state legislature from 1965 to 1977 and was elected to the U.S. Senate in 1978. As a senator, he was a leading voice in immigration reform.

Jedediah Strong Smith (1799–1831), born in New York, was a fur trader and explorer. He discovered the South Pass through the Rocky Mountains, a gateway to the Far West. He also opened the overland route to California through the Great Basin and the Sierra Nevadas and the overland trail from California to the Columbia River.

Spotted Tail (1833–81), a Lakota chief, was born near Fort Laramie. He urged compromise to avoid violence with American settlers and was a key player in his nephew Crazy Horse's surrender to the United States in 1877. Nevertheless, the Lakota were driven from their land. Spotted Tail was shot by one of his own people in 1881 for political reasons.

Spotted Tail

Francis Emroy Warren (1844–1929) was called the Dean of U.S. Senators because of his 37 years in the Senate. He was born in Massachusetts and fought in the Civil War, earning a Congressional Medal of Honor. He migrated westand was appointed governor of Wyoming Territory in 1885. In 1890, he was elected the first governor of the new state of Wyoming, but he left that office soon after to become a U.S. senator. By the end of his time in office, he had become the last Union soldier still serving in Congress.

Francis Emroy Warren

Washakie (1804?–1900), probably born in Montana, was a Shoshone chief in southwest Wyoming. He is famous for his diplomacy and for helping white settlers. He also acted as a guide to the U.S. Army for 20 years. Because of his diplomatic skill, his tribe's experience with settlers and the U.S. government was less violent than that of many other tribes.

TOUR THE STATE

Yellowstone National Park In 1872, Yellowstone became the world's first national park. It is known the world over for its hot springs and geysers including the most famous, Old Faithful, which releases steam and enormous bursts of scalding water high into the air. Wildlife, such as grizzlies, black bears, elk, moose, and bighorn sheep, thrive in this park. Be sure to visit the Grand Canyon of the Yellowstone, which is noted for its dramatic colors, and the Paintpots, large springs filled with hot clay ranging in color from white to pink to black.

Buffalo Bill Historical Center (Cody) This complex includes four museums: The Buffalo Bill Museum displays items owned by showman

Buffalo Bill Historical Center

and Pony Express rider Buffalo Bill. The Cody Firearms Museum traces the history of firearms. The Plains Indian Museum includes a large collection of Indian ceremonial artifacts and weapons. And the Whitney Gallery of Western Art contains paintings and sculptures by such famous artists as George Catlin and Frederic Remington.

Old Trail Town (Cody) Historic buildings, such as the log cabin hideout of Butch Cassidy and the Sundance Kid, have been moved to this site from throughout the state. You will also find the grave of mountain man John "Jeremiah" Smith here.

Wyoming Dinosaur Center (Thermopolis) If you love dinosaurs, this center is for you. On display are the remains of real dinosaurs, including the skeletons of triceratops—the state's official dinosaur—and a large sauropod. You can view preparation rooms to see what goes on behind the scenes of a working museum. You can also visit dig sites where crews are still uncovering dinosaur bones, talk to the crew, and even try your hand at digging up part of a dinosaur.

National Bighorn Sheep Interpretive Center (Dubois) Learn about bighorn sheep through dioramas, videos, and Sheep Mountain, a model of the animals' habitat.

Sheridan Inn (Sheridan) Built in 1892, historic Sheridan Inn was once considered the finest hotel between Chicago and San Francisco. Buffalo Bill was part-owner of this grand old building from 1894 to 1902 and auditioned acts for his world-renowned Wild West show from the front porch. It was named a National Historic Landmark in 1965.

Jim Gatchell Museum of the West (Buffalo) This regional history museum is located at the foot of the Bighorn Mountains. Jim Gatchell was a frontier pharmacist who opened a drugstore in Buffalo in 1900. The Jim Gatchell Museum features a large collection of Indian artifacts. It also houses rare, frontier-era photographs of Wyoming, as well as artifacts, tools, and weapons from nearby forts.

Devils Tower National Monument (Sundance) This unusual geological formation has sides that shoot straight up 867 feet into the air and a flat top with sagebrush and grass growing on it. You can camp, hike, or picnic nearby, or visit the prairie dog colony near the entrance. The monument was featured in the movie *Close Encounters of the Third Kind.*

Hell's Half Acre (Powder River) This area is sometimes called the Baby Grand Canyon because of its bright rocks and geological formations. The canyon is filled with great stone towers and spires.

Homesteaders Museum (Torrington) This collection of pioneer artifacts is located in a former Union Pacific Railroad depot. The museum's displays illustrate what homestead life was like from the 1880s to the 1920s.

Fort Laramie National Historic Site (Fort Laramie) Eleven buildings of this 19th-century fort have been restored, including the cavalry barracks, which housed federal troops stationed to protect settlers on their way west. During the summer, costumed guides give visitors a taste of daily military and civilian life on the post.

Cheyenne Frontier Days Old West Museum (Cheyenne) Horse-drawn wagons and other vehicles are on display here. You can also try out your rodeo skills on a mechanical bucking saddle.

Wyoming Territorial Prison and Old West Park (Laramie) Butch Cassidy and other famous outlaws once called this prison home. Also on the grounds are the National U.S. Marshal's Museum, which traces the 200-year story of the oldest federal law enforcement agency, and Frontier Town, where you can relive history by riding a stagecoach or train, watching traditional western entertainment such as puppet shows, saloon hall shows, and melodramas, or even get thrown into jail! You can also watch actors recreate the historic trial in which women served on a jury for the first time.

Independence Rock State Historic Site (Alcova) More than 5,000 explorers, adventurers, and soldiers carved their names on this well-known landmark along the Oregon Trail.

Fossil Butte National Monument (Kemmerer) Take a hike to one of the richest fossil beds in the world where you will find traces of freshwater fish that swam there more than 50 million years ago. Before setting out on your hike, you can get a close look at fossils of mammals, plants, and fish at the visitors center.

Teton Country Wagon Train (Jackson Hole) You may have a new appreciation for cars after spending four days and three nights on a wagon-train trip along the roads between Grand Teton and Yellowstone National Parks. Every night you will make camp at a new spot and settle in for dinner and song. The next day, before breaking camp, you can take canoe and horseback excursions into the countryside.

Grand Teton National Park (Jackson) This park is 485 square miles of magnificent mountainous wilderness. Lakes, glaciers, snowfields, and forests are waiting to be explored. Choose your transportation—horse, wagon, raft, canoe, or your own feet.

FUN FACTS

In 1902, Buffalo Bill Cody opened the luxurious Irma Hotel in Cody for visitors to Yellowstone. The two-story building cost $80,000. For the opening, he invited governors, ranchers, military officers, scouts, sheepherders, and other frontier people. The hundreds of guests were treated to a meal never before seen in Wyoming—scalloped oysters, shrimp and tomato salads, roast turkey, boiled ham, sliced tongue, spring chicken, fresh fruit, sugared dates, nuts, cakes, and raspberry and pineapple sherbet. He even hired an orchestra from Lincoln, Nebraska, and his guests danced until dawn.

Many place names in Wyoming have interesting origins:

The name Hell's Half Acre suggests something small, but it is actually a 320-acre area filled with unusual formations. Hell's Half Acre was once known as Devils Kitchen. According to one story, the name change was the result of a mistake by a printer. Merchants wanted to attract more tourists so they had professional pictures taken and sent them to be printed as postcards. The printer titled the image Hell's Half Acre, but the merchants used the postcards anyway.

Ten Sleep gets its name from the Indians' measure of distance by the number of "sleeps" between locations. Ten Sleep was ten sleeps from a main winter camp.

FIND OUT MORE

There are lots of interesting books and movies about Wyoming, and many ways to explore the state on the World Wide Web. Here are a few to try first.

BOOKS

State Books

Frisch, Carlienne. *Wyoming*. Minneapolis: Lerner, 1994.

Heinrichs, Ann. *America the Beautiful: Wyoming*. Chicago: Children's Press, 1992.

Sodaro, Craig, and Randy Adams. *Frontier Spirit: The Story of Wyoming*. Boulder, CO: Johnson Books, 1996.

Special Interest Books

Boehme, Sarah E. *Rendezvous to Roundup: The First One Hundred Years of Art in Wyoming*. Cody, WY: Buffalo Bill Historical Center, 1992.

Dobler, Lavinia. *Esther Morris: First Woman Justice of the Peace*. Riverton, WY: Big Bend Press, 1993.

Goodman, Susan E., and Michael J. Doolittle. *The Great Antler Auction*. New York: Atheneum, 1996. How Boy Scouts in Jackson, Wyoming, support the nearby National Elk Refuge.

Marsh, Carole. *Chill Out: Scary Wyoming Tales Based on Frightening Wyoming Truths*. Atlanta: Gallopade, 1992.

———. *Meow! Wyoming Cats in History, Mystery, Legend, Lore, Humor, and More!* Atlanta: Gallopade, 1994.

Moss, Nathaniel B. *The Shoshone Indians*. New York: Chelsea House, 1997.

Munn, Deborah. *Ghosts on the Range: Eerie True Tales of Wyoming*. Boulder, CO: Pruett, 1991.

Our Wyoming Heritage: As Seen through the Eyes of the Young. Sheridan, WY: Achievement Press, 1990.

Roberts, Phil, David L. Roberts, and Steven L. Roberts. *Wyoming Almanac*. Laramie, WY: Skyline West Press, 1994. Loaded with strange and interesting facts about Wyoming.

Fiction

O'Hara, Mary. *My Friend Flicka*. New York: HarperCollins Juvenile Books, 1988. The classic story of a boy and his horse in Wyoming.

Scott, Ann Herbert. *Brave as a Mountain Lion*. Boston: Clarion Books, 1996. Spider, a Shoshone boy, overcomes his stage fright to compete in a spelling bee.

Wallace, Bill. *Red Dog*. New York: Pocket Books, 1994. A boy defends his family's homestead in territorial Wyoming.

VIDEOS

The West. Time-Life Video, 1996. An eight-part television documentary that places Wyoming in the larger history of the American West.

Close Encounters of the Third Kind. EMI Films, 1977. The movie that made Devils Tower famous.

Butch Cassidy and the Sundance Kid. Twentieth Century Fox, 1969. Starring Paul Newman and Robert Redford.

Shane. Paramount Pictures, 1953. Homesteaders in the Tetons struggle against a villainous cattle baron.

The Virginian. Paramount Pictures, 1929. A classic Western set in Wyoming.

COMPUTER DISKS AND CD-ROMS

Marsh, Carole. *Wyoming Facts and Factivities.* CD-ROM. Atlanta: Gallopede, 1996.

———. *Wyoming: Indian Dictionary for Kids!* Computer Disk. Atlanta: Carole Marsh State Books, 1995.

WORLD WIDE WEB

http://www.uwyo.edu/Lib/Wyoming/index.html A good place to start—links to a lot of Wyoming websites.

http://www.state.wy.us/state/welcome.html Go here to find information about the government and economy of Wyoming.

http://w3.trib.com/~dont/wyoming.html Take a "virtual tour" of Wyoming from this website.

http://web66.coled.umn.edu/schools/US/Wyoming.html Links to the web-sites of Wyoming's public schools.

http://www.intermarket.com/Yellowstone/ A page devoted to everything about Yellowstone National Park.

INDEX

Chart, graph, and illustration page numbers are in boldface.